A Recipe For A Happy Author
(Which, followed closely, has made this author just that!)

Take one part of the encouragement, help, and steadfast friendship of Marjorie Fulcher, add to it the love and further reassurances of both Tom and Mary Cara, temper well with the devotion of Elvie Carson. Season with the kindness of David and all the others who have tasted and tested, and the result is this volume, for which the author gives to all his thanks and gratitude for their good wishes and patience.

Blender cookbook

by Paul Mayer

Illustrations by Craig Torlucci

A Nitty Gritty Book*
Published by
Nitty Gritty Productions
P.O. Box 5457
Concord, California 94524

*Nitty Gritty Books - Trademark
Owned by Nitty Gritty Productions
Concord, California

ISBN 0-911954-07-4

Contents

What it's all about!

The electric blender can help you to easily prepare elegant dishes, which normally take considerable time and labor, by eliminating some of the lengthy mixing procedures. For example, when using the blender to mix a cake, the butter, eggs, sugar, milk and flavorings are blended together a few seconds and then added to the flour. Cream sauces are free of lumps and egg based sauces such as hollandaise, bearnaise and mayonnaise are easily prepared without the usual problem of separating.

This book will not tell you how to make frozen daquiris, prepare frozen orange juice or any of the other everyday blender miracles you have already read about in the booklet which came with your blender. In the Blender Cookbook, I will tell you how to prepare gourmet and traditional recipes as prepared at the Paul Mayer Cooking School in San Francisco. The emphasis will be on ease of preparation with the help of a blender. I will instruct you on how to produce soups, sauces, pates, quenelles, hors d'oeuvres, vegetables and salad dressings of the highest quality.

In the great kitchens of the world, famous chefs and their helpers labor long and lovingly to create velvet-smooth pates and feather-light quenelles. By using the blender, we can re-create these delights, and many others, with relative ease. You and your family will be able to enjoy at home the dishes you have always marveled at when dining out.

Before you begin, I would like to point out a few basic lessons from my cooking school to make your life in the kitchen more pleasant and successful.

Points to remember:

Before starting any recipe, sit down and read it carefully. Be sure you have all of the ingredients and enough time to prepare the dish.

Line up ingredients and utensils in one place before starting.

Prepare equipment in advance. Be sure that all pans are buttered and floured, and that butter and chocolate are melted, if required.

Adjust racks and preheat oven to the proper temperature.

Always remember that common sense is the most important ingredient in any recipe. Don't follow along on blind faith. Your oven may be 50 degrees higher or lower than the one in the test kitchen, or your altitude may differ, or other variables may exist. Be observant and test for doneness to your own satisfaction.

And, last but not least, enjoy yourself! Cooking can be one of life's most creative and rewarding experiences.

Now, with these instructions well in mind, get out your blender and begin.

ħors d'oeuvers

Hors d'oeuvres are more than just dainty tidbits to be hand-held at cocktail parties. They are also the small but elegant first course served at the table.

In France, even a family lunch or dinner always begins with an hors d'oeuvre. Attractively arranged and decorated with bright green chopped parsley, this first course often includes leftovers from a previous meal. It is a thrifty and enjoyable method of using up yesterday's green beans, extra hard-cooked eggs, a few shrimp or the end of a roast. A thrifty French housewife also knows that a beginning course also has the advantage of making an expensive meat course go farther.

I have chosen a variety of recipes to present to you here. Many of them were collected on my trips to Europe and are my favorites. Some can be eaten out of hand, while others are more elegant and must be served on a plate with a fork, preferably at the table. You'll enjoy using your blender to make them.

5

STEAK A LA TARTARE

1/2 lb. lean round or sirloin steak
salt
3 egg yolks
1 tbs. Dijon mustard
1/4 cup olive oil

freshly ground black pepper
15 drops Worcestershire sauce
1/2 tsp. catsup
1 tbs. each parsley, capers and onion
finely chopped chives

Have butcher grind meat finely, but only once. Shape into large flat patty. Salt surface liberally. Place egg yolks, mustard, olive oil and a generous grinding of pepper in blender container. Run blender on highest speed 15 to 30 seconds or until mixture thickens and resembles mayonnaise. Remove lid. Add Worcestershire sauce, catsup, parsley, chives, capers and onion. Cover. Blend 10 seconds. Place salted meat in mixing bowl. Pour over blended mixture. Mix with hands gently but well. Shape neatly on serving dish. Sprinkle with chives. Serve raw with crackers or hot toast.

MARINATED PRAWNS

1 lb. medium-sized shrimp
1-1/3 cups olive oil
2/3 cup tarragon vinegar
salt
black pepper
paprika

1 large onion, cut in pieces
1 clove garlic
3 tbs. Dijon mustard
1 tbs. German-style mustard
2 tsp. horseradish
1 tbs. powdered thyme

Cover shrimp with salted water. Bring just to boil. Drain. Rinse under cold water to stop further cooking. Remove shells and vein. Place remaining ingredients in blender container. Blend on low speed 15 to 30 seconds or until onion is chopped. Pour over shrimp. Marinate in refrigerator overnight or until well chilled. Pour into colander. Drain off as much dressing as possible. Serve in shallow bowl. Bury a shot glass in the center. Fill with foodpicks.

SHRIMP TEMPURA

1 jar (12 oz.) chutney*	2 eggs
1/2 tsp. dry mustard	1 cup milk
2 lbs. medium sized shrimp	fat for deep frying
1 cup flour	2 to 3 tbs. flour
1/2 tsp. salt	

Place chutney and mustard in blender container. Cover. Blend on high speed until pureed. Pour into a small dish for dipping. Set aside. Shell shrimp, leaving tails attached. Split down the back but not all the way through. Remove vein. Wash and dry shrimp well. Press out flat. Wash and dry blender container. Add flour, salt, eggs, and milk. Cover. Blend on low speed until batter is completely smooth. Heat fat to 380°F. Shake dried shrimp in paper bag with 2 to 3 tablespoons flour. Dip in batter. Fry in hot fat until shrimp curl up and are crisp and golden. Serve at once with sauce.

*Crosse and Blackwell's Major Grey's Chutney

CHICKEN LIVER PATE

1 lb. fresh chicken livers
1/2 cup (1/4 lb.) butter
1 medium onion, finely chopped
salt, pepper, Tabasco
1 tsp. ground coriander
1/2 cup brandy

Place livers in a small saucepan. Barely cover with cold water. Bring slowly to boil. Reduce heat. Simmer very gently 10 minutes. Drain livers thoroughly. Place in blender container. Melt butter in small skillet. Add onion. Cook slowly without browning until soft. Put in blender container. Add salt, pepper, a drop or two of Tabasco, coriander and brandy. Cover. Blend on highest speed 30 seconds to 1 minute or until blended and smooth. Pour into crock or a mold which has been lined with aspic. If you do use an aspic lined mold, be sure the pate is well chilled before adding, lest you melt the aspic. Chill. Press plastic wrap firmly against surface of pate to prevent it from drying.

9

SARDINE-STUFFED LEMONS

6 lemons
2 cans (3-3/4 oz. each) sardines
5 oz. (10 tbs.) butter
1 tbs. Dijon mustard
paprika, pepper
1/2 tsp. crushed thyme

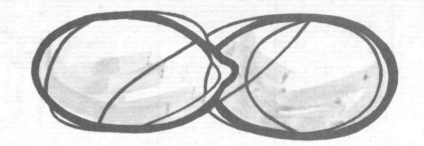

Cut tops from lemons. Scoop out the pulp using a grapefruit knife. Place sardines, butter and mustard in blender container. Cover. Blend on high speed until mixture is well pureed. Season with paprika, pepper, a little lemon juice and pulp and thyme. Blend on high speed 10 to 15 seconds. Fill lemon shells with mixture using a pastry tube with large star tip if available. Chill mixture thoroughly. Garnish each star with a caper. Serve with crackers or hot buttered toast.

CANAPE DE LA MER

1/2 cup blanched almonds
1 can (6-1/2 oz.) minced clams
2 tbs. chives
1 cup mayonnaise
2 egg whites
8 slices bread

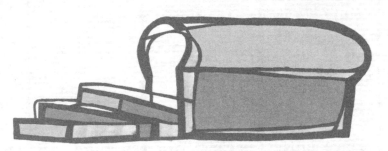

Place almonds in blender container. Cover. Run on low speed until nuts are pulverized. Empty into a mixing bowl. Add clams and chives to blender container. Cover. Blend on low speed until clams are finely chopped. Add to nuts. Stir in mayonnaise. Beat egg whites until stiff. Fold into mayonnaise mixture. Toast bread on one side only. Spread untoasted side with clam mixture. Wet a sharp knife. Trim crusts and cut toast into squares. Run under broiler until topping is puffed and browned.

TOAST SUR NOISETTES

1/2 cup (1/4 lb.) soft butter
1 cup pecans
few drops Worcestershire sauce
1/2 tsp. catsup
8 slices bread

Place butter, pecans, Worcestershire and catsup in blender container. Cover. Blend on low speed until nuts are ground and well mixed with butter. If mixture is too soft, chill briefly. Toast bread on one side only. Spread untoasted side with butter mixture. Run under broiler until nuts are toasted and nicely browned. Cut into strips or squares. Serve at once.

CANAPE DE FROMAGE

6 slices bacon
2 tbs. butter
2 tbs. flour
garlic salt, cayenne
1/2 cup cream

1 cup Gruyere cheese chunks
1/2 small onion
1 beaten egg
paprika, Dijon mustard, Worcestershire sauce
8 slices bread

Cook bacon until very crisp. Drain well. Place bacon, butter, flour, garlic salt, cayenne, cream, Gruyere and onion in blender container. Cover. Blend on high speed until cheese is grated, about 30 seconds. Pour into saucepan. Stir over moderate heat until sauce thickens and boils and cheese is melted. Do not be alarmed if it is over-buttery at this point. Add beaten egg. Season with paprika, mustard and a little Worcestershire sauce. Spread on flat plate. Cover with plastic wrap. Chill. Trim crusts from bread. Toast on one side only. Spread untoasted side with softened butter and toast. Cool. Spread generously with chilled cheese mixture. Sprinkle with paprika. Cut into strips or squares. Run under the broiler until crusty and browned. Serve hot!

13

HOT STUFFED ARTICHOKE LEAVES

Instead of using bread as a base or holder for your fillings, you might like to try these.

cooked artichoke leaves
1 jar (5 oz.) boned chicken <u>or</u>
5 oz. cooked lobster

1/2 small onion
1 to 2 tbs. mayonnaise
marjoram, salt, pepper

Handle artichoke leaves carefully so that the meaty end of the leaf remains intact. Place meat, onion, mayonnaise, salt and pepper in blender container. Cover. Blend on low speed 30 seconds. Place a small amount of the mixture on the meaty end of the artichoke leaves. Pipe mayonnaise through a pastry tube so as to cover the filling completely. Run under the broiler until mayonnaise is puffed and browned. Serve hot.

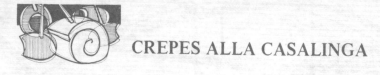

CREPES ALLA CASALINGA

Now, some hors d'oeuvres which are not canapes! These require a fork and definitely must be served on a plate, preferably at the table.

Blender Crepes, page 156
4 oz. Gruyere cheese
4 oz. imported Parmesan cheese
3 tbs. butter
5 tbs. flour

salt, cayenne pepper
1 cup milk
1 cup (1/2 pt.) whipping cream
1/8 tsp. dry mustard
Sauce Casalinga, page 17

Prepare crepes as directed. Cook using a 10 inch crepe pan. Make as many as batter will permit. Cut cheese in small chunks. Place in blender container with butter, flour, salt, pepper, milk, cream and dry mustard. Cover. Blend on high speed until cheese is grated and sauce well blended, about 30 to 60 seconds. Pour into pan. Stir over moderate heat until it becomes very thick and boils. Spread mixture on a large flat plate. Press plastic wrap down on surface to prevent drying. Chill until thickened and very cold. Spread each pancake with some of the

16

cheese mixture. Roll up and cut on the bias into pieces 1 inch wide. Each crepe should yield about 6 pieces. Pack pieces on their pin wheel sides into an oven proof baking dish. Cover with Casalinga Sauce. Place dish in 425°F oven for at least 10 minutes or until the whole dish is sizzling. Serve immediately.

SAUCE CASALINGA

1 pkg. dried Italian style mushrooms
1 tbs. olive oil

1 tsp. tomato paste
1 cup strong beef stock

Soak mushrooms in water at least 1 hour. After crepes are filled and cut, drain mushrooms. Dry thoroughly. Chop finely. Heat olive oil in a skillet. Cook mushrooms quickly, about 1 minute. Remove from heat. Stir in tomato paste and stock (either homemade or made by dissolving 1-1/4 teaspoons Boveril in 1 cup hot water). Place pan over heat again. Quickly reduce sauce until it measures one half its original quantity. Use as directed.

BEURRECK DRAP D'OR

When I first went to Europe in 1960, one of the places recommended was a small restaurant in Cannes, Le Drap d'Or, where I was served some of the most delicious hors d'oeuvers ever. This is one of their specialties.

Blender Crepes, page 156
2 tbs. butter
3 tbs. flour
1-1/4 cups half and half
6 oz. Gruyere cheese
salt, white pepper, nutmeg
1 egg
1 tsp. water
flour, bread crumbs
deep fat for frying

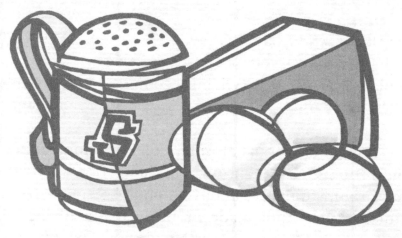

Cook crepes in 5 inch pan. Stack and set aside. Place butter, flour, half and

18

half, cheese and seasonings in blender container. Cover. Blend on high speed about 30 seconds, or until cheese is grated. Pour mixture into saucepan. Stir over moderate heat until mixture boils and cheese is melted. Transfer sauce to a shallow bowl. Cover surface closely with plastic wrap. Chill well. Place a spoonful of chilled mixture on each crepe. Fold in such a way as to make a square package. Seal well. Beat egg and water together. Dip folded crepes in flour, then in egg. Coat well with crumbs. Allow crepes to dry about 30 minutes. Heat fat to 380°F. Fry crepes until crisp and deeply browned. Drain on paper towels. Serve at once before cheese can solidify. Makes 18. Serve 1 per person for hors d'oeuvres, 2 or 3 for luncheon.

CROQUE-MONSIEUR

1/2 lb. Gruyere cheese	9 thin ham slices
whipping cream	3 eggs
18 slices of bread	3 tbs. water

Cut cheese into small pieces. Place in blender container. Cover. Blend on medium speed until cheese is grated. Remove cover. Slowly pour in enough cream to make a paste which will spread easily but not run. Lay bread slices in such a fashion as to have every other one opposing its neighbors so when closed the slices will match. Spread each slice with a thin layer of cheese mixture. On 9 slices place a slice of ham. Close sandwiches. Trim off crusts. Cut each into 4 triangular pieces by slicing from corner to corner. Lightly grease a heavy skillet. Heat. Combine eggs and water. Dip each sandwich triangle. Fry on each side until nicely browned. Let rest a minute or two before serving to allow cheese to set slightly. If desired, serve with the following sauce. Makes 36 triangles.

2 tbs. butter
2 tbs. flour
1 cup (1/2 pint) whipping cream
salt, dry mustard
2 egg yolks

Place butter, flour, cream, salt and mustard in blender container. Cover. Blend on medium speed until well mixed. Pour into saucepan. Stir over moderate heat until mixture boils. Beat egg yolks. Add a little of the hot sauce, beating rapidly. Return to saucepan. Stir briskly until sauce thickens. Pour into serving dish. Dust with paprika. Arrange sandwich triangles on platter. Garnish with parsley. Pass sauce with sandwiches.

Soups

I love soups and I enjoy preparing them the easy blender way.

Soups make perfect meal starters. A cup of soup whets the appetite for the meal to follow like nothing else can. When soup is served at the beginning of a meal, the salad is usually served following the entree where it serves to clear the palate and prepare it for what comes next. This is typical of French meals and preferred by many Americans.

Bowls of steaming hot soup are extremely inviting on a chilly day or as a late night supper. Equally enjoyable are iced soups on a warm summer day. No matter what the season, a wholesome, delicious meal can be built around a hearty soup, crusty bread and a salad. Fruit and cheese make a fine finish.

Once you've seen how easily soups can be made with the help of a blender, you'll start brightening up your meals with these favorites.

23

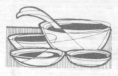

ALMOND SOUP

3/4 cup blanched almonds
2-1/2 cups chicken broth
1/2 onion, unsliced
1 bay leaf
1 cup (1/2 pint) whipping cream
1/2 tsp. ground coriander

2 tbs. butter
2 tbs. flour
salt to taste
1 to 2 drops almond extract
slivers of toasted almonds for garnish

Place almonds and broth in blender container. Cover. Run blender on medium speed about 30 seconds, or until nuts are ground. Pour mixture into saucepan with onion and bay leaf. Bring to boil. Simmer, uncovered 20 minutes. Remove from heat. Discard onion and bay leaf. Slowly add cream and coriander. Return pan to heat. Simmer 5 minutes. Knead butter and flour together with hands until absolutely smooth. Add this "beurre manie" (kneaded butter) to the simmering soup. Allow to cook 1 minute. Stir to thoroughly blend. Add salt to taste and almond extract, if desired. Serve hot, garnished with slivers of toasted almonds. Makes 4 to 6 servings.

CHILLED CAVIAR SOUP

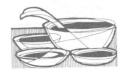

At the going rate for caviar, you may not want to splurge on this, but actually, each grain is a worthy addition to this most glamorous of cold soups.

2 tbs. butter
2 tbs. flour
2 cups rich chicken broth
salt, white pepper to taste

1 tbs. lemon juice
1 cup (1/2 pint) whipping cream
2 tbs. REAL caviar

Place butter, flour and broth in blender container. Add salt and a small amount of pepper. Cover. Blend 15 to 30 seconds on highest speed. Pour into saucepan. Stir over medium heat until mixture boils. Reduce heat. Cook slowly until soup thickens. Remove from heat. Add lemon juice, 1 teaspoon at a time, to suit your individual taste. Stir in cream. Correct seasoning. Chill thoroughly. Just before serving, add caviar. Stir carefully through soup.

Note: If using caviar from a jar, rinse it well using cold water.

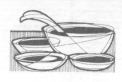

ICED CREAM OF ARTICHOKE SOUP

At the very westernmost part of Austria, on the shores of Lake Constance, is the town of Bergenz. Just a "katzenspring" from both Germany and Switzerland, yet it retains its Austrian flavor. It was there, at the Hotel Weisses Kreuz, I enjoyed a magnificent dinner which left me gasping in its elegance. It began with this soup.

5 or 6 large artichokes	6 tbs. butter
lemon	6 tbs. flour
1 tsp. salt	1 to 2 cups whipping cream
tarragon vinegar	3 tbs. chopped garlic dill pickle
3 to 4 peppercorns	whipped cream for garnish

Trim tops and stems from artichokes. Rub cuts with lemon. Set, single layer, in large pan. Barely cover with water. Add salt, a dash of vinegar and peppercorns. Cook at least 1-1/2 hours or until over-soft and leaves are falling off. Lift artichokes from pan and drain. Reserve cooking liquid. Scrape as much pulp from

26

leaves as possible. Remove chokes and trim hearts. Place hearts and scraped pulp in blender container with as much of the cooking liquid as the blender will hold comfortably. Cover. Run blender 15 to 30 seconds, or until pulp is pureed and blended with liquid. Add butter and flour. Cover. Blend 15 seconds or until contents are well mixed. Pour into saucepan. Stir over medium heat until mixture boils. If too thick, thin slightly with a bit more cooking liquid. Add cream until cooked mixture is the consistency of a thickened split pea soup. Add chopped pickle. Reheat. Serve steaming hot. Garnish each serving with a spoonful of whipped cream. Makes 4 to 6 servings.

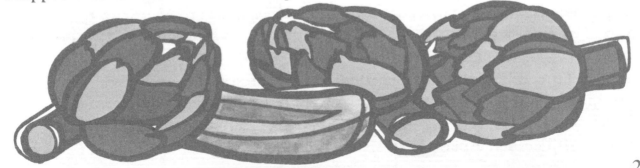

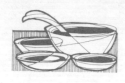

ICED CREAM OF ASPARAGUS & CRAB SOUP

2 lbs. fresh asparagus
1 bunch green onions, thinly sliced
2 tbs. butter
pinch marjoram
salt, white pepper

5 to 6 tbs. water
5 tbs. flour
2 cups chicken stock
1 cup (1/2 pt.) whipping cream
1/4 lb. fresh crab meat

Cut tips from asparagus. Cook tips only, 3 to 4 minutes in boiling water. Drain well. Chill. Wash remaining stalks. Discard tough ends. Cut stalks into 2-inch slices. Place in saucepan with onions. Add butter, marjoram, a little salt and pepper. Heat until butter is melted. Toss vegetables to coat with butter. Add water. Cover pan tightly. Cook slowly until asparagus is tender. Remove from heat. Force mixture through strainer or Foley Food Mill to remove stringy pieces. Place puree in blender container. Add flour and stock. Cover. Run blender on high speed 15 to 30 seconds. Pour into saucepan. Stir over brisk heat until mixture boils. Correct seasoning. Add cream and crab meat. Chill. Serve icy cold. Garnish with chilled asparagus tips. Makes 4 to 6 servings.

POTAGE CREME NIVERNAISE

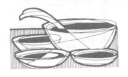

7 to 8 carrots	1/4 cup flour
1/4 cup butter	salt, cayenne pepper
1 tsp. sugar	2-1/2 cups milk
1/2 tsp. salt	1/2 cup whipping cream
1/4 cup water	parsley or mint

Peel and slice carrots. Melt 2 tablespoons butter in saucepan. Add carrots, sugar, salt and water. Cover. Cook slowly 20 minutes. Remove a few carrot slices for garnish. Add remaining butter to pan. Stir until melted. Remove from heat. Add flour, salt and cayenne to taste. Stir in milk. Cook over medium heat, stirring constantly, until soup boils. Reduce heat. Cook slowly until thick, at least 25 minutes. Put thickened mixture into blender container. Cover. Blend on highest speed 15 to 30 seconds, or until velvety smooth. Return to saucepan. Add cream and reserved carrot slices. Reheat. Serve steaming hot. Garnish with parsley or finely chopped mint. Makes 4 to 6 servings.

ICED CREAM OF CUCUMBER SOUP

3 large cucumbers
2 tbs. melted butter
2 whole shallots
6 tbs. flour
3 cups chicken broth
1 cup milk, scalded

2 to 3 sprigs mint
1/2 cup whipping cream
salt, white pepper
sour cream
cucumber slices
chopped mint

Peel, seed and coarsely chop cucumbers. Place in blender container with butter and shallots. Blend on medium speed 15 to 30 seconds. Pour into saucepan. Cook slowly 20 minutes. Return mixture to blender container. Add flour, chicken broth, milk and mint sprigs. Cover. Blend until ingredients are thoroughly blended. Return to saucepan. Stir over moderate heat until soup boils. Add cream. Season to taste with salt and pepper. Chill thoroughly. Serve garnished with sour cream, unpeeled cucumber slices and chopped mint. Makes 4 to 6 servings.

TOMATO AND DILL SOUP

This soup is equally good served hot or cold.

2 tbs. vegetable oil
1 tbs. butter
1 onion, finely sliced
1 clove garlic
salt, black pepper
3 large tomatoes, sliced

1 can (6 oz.) tomato paste
6 tbs. flour
2 cups water
3/4 cup cream, whipped
1 tbs. finely minced fresh dill or
1 tbs. dried dill weed

Heat oil and butter in saucepan. Add onion, garlic, salt and pepper. Cook slowly until onion is soft. Increase heat. Add tomato slices. Cook briskly 3 minutes. Remove from heat. Add tomato paste and flour. Stir in water. Return to medium heat. Stir constantly until mixture comes to a full boil. Rub through a fine strainer. Pour into blender container. Cover. Blend on high speed 15 to 30 seconds. Return to pan. Add cream and dill. Reheat and serve. Also, delicious served well-chilled. Makes 4 to 6 servings.

POTAGE CREME DE ROMAINE

2 heads romaine lettuce
2 tbs. butter
1/4 cup chopped onion
1/4 cup flour
salt, freshly ground pepper

3-3/4 cups milk
1 tsp. Arrowroot
1/2 cup whipping cream
Freshly Made Croutons, page 33
finely chopped mint

Wash romaine well. Shred it. Melt butter in deep saucepan. Add lettuce and onion. Cover. Stew gently 7 minutes. Remove from heat. Add flour. Season with salt and pepper. Carefully stir in milk. Return to heat. Stir constantly until soup boils. Reduce heat. Simmer 20 minutes. Pour half of mixture into blender container. Cover. Blend until smooth, 15 to 30 seconds. Pour into saucepan. Repeat with remaining soup. Dissolve Arrowroot in whipping cream. Stir into soup. Bring to boil. Serve piping hot topped with freshly made croutons and finely chopped mint. Makes 4 to 6 servings.

oil
firm white bread slices

Pour enough oil into a skillet to float the number of croutons you are making. Heat to 375° to 390°. Cut slices of bread into small cubes. Drop cubes, all at once, into hot oil. Remove as soon as they begin to brown. Drain on absorbent paper. It is desirable to make only enough croutons for immediate use as they become rancid quickly. If necessary, store in tightly sealed jar.

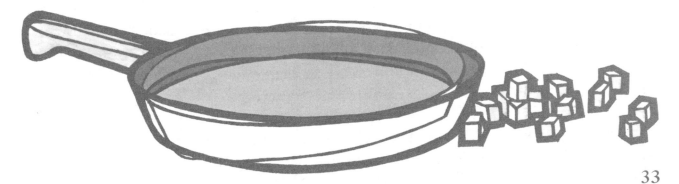

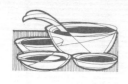

CREME HAMILTON

1/2 lb. mushrooms	1/4 cup milk	finely chopped chives*
3 tbs. butter	1/2 cup cream, whipped	
2 tsp. potato starch	whipped cream for garnish	

Place mushrooms in blender container. Cover. Blend on low speed 30 seconds, or until mushrooms are coarsely chopped. Place in saucepan. Allow to stew gently over low heat until mushrooms are very soft. Remove from heat, add 2 tablespoons butter. Stir until melted. Return to blender. Add remaining butter and potato starch (sometimes called potato flour). Blend on highest speed 15 to 30 seconds, or until completely smooth. Pour back into saucepan. Stir over moderate heat until soup boils. It will be very thick. Add milk. Gently fold in whipped cream. This is a rich soup. Serve in demi-tasse cups, topped with a tiny bit of whipped cream and chives. Makes 4 to 6 servings.

*I find the Armanino freeze dried chives completely acceptable for every dish requiring chives in any form.

CREAM OF ONION SOUP

8 onions
1/4 cup butter
6 tbs. flour
salt, cayenne pepper, to taste

2 cups hot milk
1 to 2 cups (1/2 to 1 pt.) whipping cream
Gruyere cheese, grated
nutmeg

Slice onions. Place in pan. Barely cover with boiling water. Cook slowly until onions are tender. Place in blender container. Cover. Blend 15 to 30 seconds. Add butter, flour, salt, cayenne and milk. Cover. Blend on highest speed 15 to 30 seconds. Pour into saucepan. Stir over medium heat until mixture boils. Remove from heat. Thin to desired consistency with cream. Correct seasoning. Reheat. Allow to simmer gently 3 minutes. Pour into flame-proof tureen. Sprinkle surface with grated Gruyere cheese and a dash of nutmeg. Run under hot broiler until cheese glazes and begins to crust. Serve at once. Makes 4 to 6 servings.

POTAGE SIMON

2 bunches carrots
6 tbs. butter
salt, cayenne pepper
1 tbs. sugar
1-1/2 cups water

2 bunches spinach
1/2 cup flour
1 cup chicken broth
3 cups milk

Peel and slice carrots. Melt butter in deep saucepan. Add carrots, salt, cayenne and sugar. Stir to coat carrots. Add water. Cover. Cook slowly for 5 minutes. Add well-washed spinach. Cook, covered, until carrots are soft. Remove from heat. Pour contents into blender container. Add flour, broth and milk. Cover. Blend at highest speed 15 to 30 seconds. Return soup to saucepan. Cook, stirring constantly until it boils. If too thick, thin with additional milk. Correct seasoning. Serve hot. Makes 4 to 6 servings.

For a Polynesian-type soup, add 1 to 2 tablespoons Japanese oyster sauce. Serve in oven-proof dishes. Top with whipped cream. Run under the broiler until cream has melted and turned brown. Serve sizzling.

36

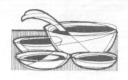

VICHYSOISSE

I guess by now everyone knows that vichysoisse is not truly a French soup, but was originated in the kitchens of the old Ritz-Carlton hotel in New York by the master of chefs, Louis Diat!

4 potatoes
1 bunch large leeks
2 tbs. butter

salt, cayenne pepper
2-1/2 cups water
2 cups milk

1 cup (1/2 pt.) whipping cream
2 to 3 tbs. chives

Peel and thinly slice potatoes and leeks. Melt butter in saucepan. Add potatoes, leeks, salt and cayenne. Turn vegetables about in butter to glaze. Add 1-1/2 cups water. Cover pan. Cook over medium heat until potatoes are soft and mushy. Add remaining water and milk. Stir until mixture comes to boil. Set off heat 10 minutes. Pour soup into blender container. Cover. Blend on highest speed 15 to 30 seconds. Add cream and chives. Chill thoroughly. If too thick, thin to desired consistency with milk. It should be thin enough for the chives to float. Vichysoisse is always served icy cold. Makes 4 to 6 servings.

POTATO AND WATERCRESS SOUP

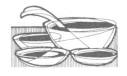

4 medium potatoes*
1 medium onion
2 tbs. butter
1 cup water

salt, white pepper to taste
2 bunches watercress
1 cup (1/2 pt.) whipping cream

Peel and thinly slice potatoes and onion. Melt butter in deep saucepan. Add vegetables. Toss to coat with butter. Add water, salt and pepper. Cover pan. Cook slowly until potatoes are thoroughly soft. Coarsely chop 1 bunch watercress. Add to potato mixture. Stir until soup boils. Remove from heat. Pour into blender container. Cover. Blend on highest speed 15 to 30 seconds or until mixture is smooth. Return to saucepan. Remove leaves from remaining bunch of watercress. Add leaves and cream to soup. Correct seasoning. Heat to serving temperature. Serve steaming. Makes 4 to 6 servings.

*preferably not Idahos

BISQUE OF LIMA BEANS AND CHAMPAGNE

Caviar before, champagne now, and this one takes its place among the most elegant of all the soups.

1/4 cup butter
1 small onion, quartered
1 pkg. (10 oz.) Fordhook lima beans
2 cups water
2 tbs. flour
1 egg yolk
3/4 cup whipping cream
salt, pepper
2 cups champagne

Melt 2 tablespoons butter in large saucepan. Pour into blender container. Add onion quarters. Cover. Blend 15 to 30 seconds on low speed. Pour mixture into saucepan. Cook slowly until onion is soft, but not browned. Add lima beans and

40

water. Bring to boil. Add a pinch of salt and thyme. (A pinch, by the way, is what you can take between your thumb and index finger.) Continue cooking slowly until beans are very soft. Force mixture through a pureeing device such as a Foley Food Mill. Pour lima bean puree into blender container. Add flour and remaining butter. Cover. Blend at highest speed 15 to 30 seconds. Pour into saucepan. Blend egg yolk and cream together well. Place saucepan over medium heat. Stir mixture until it is boiling. Remove from heat. Add cream slowly, stirring frantically all the time. Keep soup hot, without permitting it to boil. Season it highly with salt and pepper—even more than seems sufficient. Just before serving, add champagne. Reheat swiftly so foam from champagne will not be lost completely. Serve as hot as possible. Makes 4 to 6 servings.

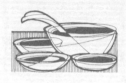

CREAM OF SAFFRON SOUP

1-1/2 cups diced potatoes
1 cup chopped celery
1 cup chopped onion
2 cups milk
salt, white pepper, to taste
1/4 tsp. saffron
1 cup (1/2 pt.) cream
black caviar

Combine vegetables in saucepan. Add milk. Cook over medium heat 10 minutes, or until tender. Pour mixture into blender container. Add salt, pepper and saffron. Cover. Blend on highest speed 15 to 30 seconds. Pour into metal bowl. Add cream. Chill thoroughly. When serving, place a good spoonful of caviar in each soup plate after ladling in the soup. Makes 4 to 6 servings.

1 tbs. butter
2 tbs. vegetable oil
1 onion, finely chopped
1 clove garlic
2 pkg. (10 oz. ea.) frozen peas
salt, pepper

1 scant tbs. curry powder
2-1/2 tbs. flour
2 cups chicken broth
1/2 to 1 cup (1/2 pt.) whipping cream
2/3 cup chicken, finely minced

Heat butter and oil together. Add onion and garlic. Cook slowly, 3 minutes. Add peas, salt, pepper and curry. Continue cooking slowly until peas are soft. Remove from heat. Blend in flour. Stir in broth. Return to heat. Stir until soup boils. Force mixture through Foley Food Mill. Pour into blender container. Cover. Blend on highest speed until smooth, 30 to 45 seconds. Return to pan. Thin with cream to desired consistency. Stir in chicken. Reheat and serve. Excellent thinned with milk and served well chilled. Makes 4 to 6 servings.

Egg Dishes

Hundreds of egg recipes can be prepared using the blender. I have selected a few well known favorites and some new ones, the preparation of which is greatly aided by the blender. I am also including some cooking suggestions and information which my students have found helpful.

Let us begin with instructions for poaching eggs since many people think they are tricky, time consuming and must be done at the last minute. Actually, poached eggs are none of the former and I encourage you to use them often. Let's tackle the last-minute bit first! Believe it or not, poached eggs can be kept successfully in a large bowl of tap water as hot as your hand can stand, if you keep replenishing the water as it cools. The easiest way to ensure perfectly shaped poached eggs is to be sure that the eggs you use are fresh since the older the egg, the less your chances of success. By following these simple instructions, I can

45

guarantee you will serve nicely shaped poached eggs everytime.

To properly poach an egg, fill a large, lightly greased skillet 2/3 full with hot water. Add a little salt and 1 teaspoon of white vinegar. Bring to a full boil. Have the eggs ready—either at room temperature or warmed by running them briefly under the hot tap water. Place the UNOPENED eggs in the boiling water for 10 seconds. (An easy way to count seconds is "one-Mississippi, two-Mississippi, three-Mississippi, etc.). After 10 Mississippis, remove the eggs from the boiling water. Lower the heat until the water is barely simmering. Carefully break the eggs directly into the water. After the last egg has been broken, increase the heat until the water is once again barely simmering. Allow the eggs to poach for an additional 4 minutes. Gently lift eggs from the pan with a slotted spoon. Place them on absorbent paper to drain, or drop them into a bowl of hot water as described on page 45. And, that's all there is to it!

Now, let's explore some poached egg dishes.

EGGS BENEDICT

6 eggs
2 egg yolks
2 tbs. lemon juice
salt, cayenne pepper, to taste
1/2 cup hot, melted butter
6 English muffin halves
6 thin slices ham or Canadian bacon
truffles or black olives

Poach eggs and keep warm as directed on page 46 while making Hollandaise Sauce. Combine egg yolks, lemon juice, salt and cayenne in blender container. Cover. Blend on low speed until mixture is turning freely in blades. Slowly pour in hot butter. Continue blending only until sauce thickens. Toast and butter muffin halves and saute ham in dry skillet. Assemble dish by placing a slice of ham on top of each muffin. Drain and dry eggs carefully. Place on ham. Spoon sauce over all. Garnish with thin slices of truffle or black olives. Makes 6 servings.

ARTICHAUD EN COCOTTE SURPRISE

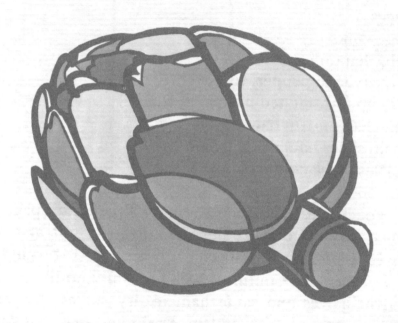

6 artichokes
3 to 4 tbs. tarragon vinegar
3 tbs. olive oil
4 to 5 peppercorns
1 bay leaf
6 eggs
5 tbs. butter
pate de foie gras
1/4 cup flour
salt, freshly ground pepper
1/2 cup tomato juice
1/4 cup milk
1/2 cup sour cream
marjoram

Trim thorny tips from artichoke leaves. Boil artichokes in plenty of salted water with vinegar, olive oil, peppercorns and bay leaf added. Cook until leaves come away with a little of the meat from the heart, when pulled gently. Remove artichokes from water. Drain until cool enough to handle. Pull out all center leaves. Remove choke by scraping it out with a teaspoon. Invert to drain. Poach eggs. Keep hot in a bowl of water as directed on page 46. Remove leaves from artichokes. Set aside. Trim hearts. Saute in 3 tablespoons butter until nicely browned on both sides. Place in 6 individual ramekins or cocottes. Top each heart with a slice of pate de foie gras. Keep warm. Place remaining 2 tablespoons butter, flour, salt, pepper, tomato juice and milk in blender container. Cover. Blend at high speed 15 to 30 seconds. Pour into saucepan. Stir over moderate heat until mixture boils. Add sour cream to thin to spreading consistency. Add marjoram to taste. Drain and dry eggs on paper towels. Place one egg in each ramekin on top of pate. Coat eggs with sauce. Rebuild artichokes by replacing the leaves about each heart in such a manner as to resemble a whole artichoke.

LES OEUFS POCHES ELYSEE

6 patty shells
Poulet en Sauce Creme, page 51
Sauce Hollandaise, page 171
6 poached eggs
6 slices Canadian bacon
thin truffle slices

Patty shells ready for baking can be found in the frozen bread section of most supermarkets. Bake according to directions. Prepare creamed chicken and Hollandaise Sauce. Poach eggs and keep warm in a bowl of hot water as described on page 46. Saute bacon slices. When ready to serve, fill patty shells half way with creamed chicken. Place bacon on top of chicken. Drain and dry eggs. Place on top of bacon. Mask eggs with Hollandaise. Garnish with truffle slices. Makes 6 servings.

POULET EN SAUCE CREME

meat from 1 stewed chicken
1/4 cup butter
6 tbs. flour
1 cup chicken broth
1 cup milk
1 cup (1/2 pt.) cream
salt, cayenne pepper
4 egg yolks
1/4 tsp. paprika

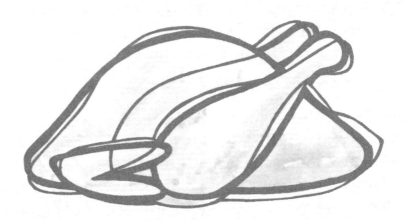

Cut chicken into fair-sized bits. Measure butter, flour, broth, milk, cream, salt and cayenne into blender container. Cover. Blend on highest speed 15 to 30 seconds. Pour into large saucepan. Stir over medium heat until mixture boils. Remove from heat. Quickly beat in egg yolks. Stir over lowest heat to cook eggs. Do not allow to boil. Add paprika. Correct seasonings. Stir in chicken and heat, stirring constantly. Use as directed.

SOUFFLES

You can easily avoid the disappointment of a souffle which fails to rise, or even worse, falls flat on its way to the table. Consistantly successful souffles are easy to accomplish once you understand what goes on in the process of making one.

It is air that causes the souffle to rise. Think of the stiffly beaten egg whites as hundreds of tiny balloons. When the air inside these little balloons is heated in the oven it expands, the balloons blow up and the souffle rises. Just as over inflated balloons will burst, the egg white balloons will burst if you leave the souffle in the oven too long because heat creates overexpansion and the skins become brittle.

Most American cookbooks call for cooking souffles too long. For a six cup souffle dish and a 375° oven, 17 minutes is ample. A good souffle makes its own sauce and it is the dry souffles which are failures.

Souffles fall into two categories. In the first type, which includes cheese, chocolate, vegetable and meaty souffles, the base is not brought to the boiling point. In the second group, which includes all fruit and liqueur souffles, the base is brought to a full boil to thicken it before adding the egg yolks and flavorings. It

52

is necessary to start with a thick base since the additon of fruit or liqueur thins it considerably. The stiffly beaten egg whites are always folded into the base, never the other way around. This will mean transferring the base to a large bowl before adding the whites, but the success of your souffle may well depend upon your using that extra bowl.

ASPARAGUS SOUFFLE

6 cup, well-buttered souffle dish
1 lb. asparagus (approximately)
3 tbs. butter
1 small onion, quartered
3 tbs. flour

3/4 cup milk
salt, cayenne pepper
4 egg yolks
6 egg whites
Parmesan cheese

Preheat oven to 375°F. Cook asparagus in boiling, salted water. Drain. Puree a few pieces at a time, using blender, until there is 1 cup puree in blender container. Add butter, onion, flour and milk. Cover. Blend on high speed 30 seconds. Pour into saucepan. Season with salt and cayenne. Cook over moderate heat, stirring until mixture begins to thicken. Remove from heat. Stir briskly to stop further cooking. Beat in egg yolks, one at a time. Correct seasoning. Turn into large bowl. Fold in egg whites which have been beaten until stiff, but not dry. Pour batter into prepared dish. Sprinkle lightly with Parmesan. Bake in preheated oven 17 to 18 minutes. Serve immediately. Makes 4 to 6 servings.

CARROT SOUFFLE

6 cup, well-buttered souffle dish
1 lb. carrots (approximately)
3 tbs. butter
1 small onion
3 tbs. flour

3/4 cup milk
salt, cayenne pepper
4 eggs yolks
6 egg whites
Parmesan cheese

Preheat oven to 375°F. Peel and slice carrots. Cook in boiling salted water. Drain. Puree carrot slices, a few at a time, until there is 1 cup puree in blender container. Add butter, onion, which has been cut into pieces, flour and milk. Cover. Blend on high speed 30 seconds. Pour into saucepan. Season with salt and cayenne. Cook over moderate heat, stirring until mixture begins to thicken. Remove from heat. Stir rapidly to stop any further cooking. Beat in egg yolks, one at a time. Correct seasoning. Turn into large bowl. Fold in egg whites which have been beaten until stiff, but not dry. Pour batter into prepared dish. Sprinkle lightly with Parmesan. Bake in preheated oven 17 to 18 minutes. Makes 4 to 6 servings.

SPINACH SOUFFLE

6 cup, well-buttered souffle dish
1 bunch spinach
3 tbs. butter
1 small onion, quartered

3 tbs. flour
3/4 cup milk
salt, cayenne pepper, to taste
pinch nutmeg

4 egg yolks
7 egg whites

Preheat oven to 375° F. Wash spinach well. Remove stems. If left on, they are apt to wrap around the shaft of the blender, damaging the motor. Put spinach in pot with only the water clinging to it after washing. Cook just until wilted. Drain well. Rinse in cold water. Squeeze small handfuls tightly until spinach is free of water. Chop coarsely. Place in blender container. Add butter, onion, flour, milk, salt, cayenne and nutmeg. Cover. Blend on highest speed 15 to 30 seconds. Pour mixture into saucepan. Stir over moderate heat until mixture begins to thicken. Remove from heat. Stir rapidly to prevent further cooking. Beat in egg yolks, one at a time. Turn batter into large bowl. Fold in egg whites which have been beaten until stiff, but not dry. Pour into prepared dish. Bake in preheated oven 17 to 18 minutes. Serve immediately. Makes 4 to 6 servings.

56

CHEDDAR CHEESE SOUFFLE

6 cup, well-buttered souffle dish
2 tbs. butter
2 tbs. flour
3/4 cup milk
4 oz. sharp, Cheddar cheese
salt, cayenne pepper
4 egg yolks
6 egg whites

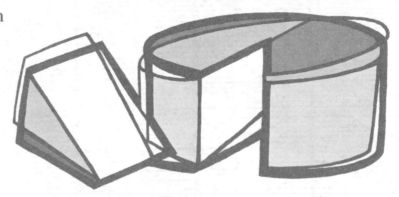

Preheat oven to 375°F. Into blender container put butter, flour, milk, salt, cayenne and cheese, which has been broken into pieces. Cover. Blend on highest speed 30 seconds. Pour mixture into saucepan. Stir over moderate heat until sauce just begins to thicken. Remove from heat. Beat in egg yolks, one at a time. Turn into large bowl. Fold in egg whites which have been beaten until stiff, but not dry. Pour into prepared dish. Bake in preheated oven 17 to 18 minutes. Serve immediately. Makes 4 to 6 servings.

Fish & Shellfish

    We used to eat fish because it was inexpensive, or Friday, but today neither of these reasons is valid. I am surprised to find that many people do not like fish and I feel that this is simply because they have never tasted it properly prepared.

    Fish and shellfish are delicate and should be handled with gentleness. They may be fried, baked, broiled, poached or sauteed, but always with care. The best way to cook a certain kind of fish depends on whether it is fat, or lean and dry. Fat fish such as salmon, halibut, rock cod, red snapper and albacore are usually baked or broiled. Lean fish are most delicious when fried or poached and served with a delicate sauce. Sole, flounder, trout and swordfish are among those classified as lean. Shellfish of all kinds are rich in flavor and are usually prepared so as not to obscure their character. Avoid heavy sauces, long cooking and high temperature for all fish.

STUFFED FISH A LA CLUB BARRANQUELLA

4 cups firm bread cubes
4 lb. whole red snapper
garlic salt, pepper
1 lb. blanched almonds
6 tbs. butter
3 tbs. finely chopped onion
1/4 tsp. salt
1 large peeled cucumber
pinch ground cloves, pepper
1 tsp. sage
1/4 cup dry white wine
bacon
melted butter-white wine

Allow bread cubes to dry, uncovered, overnight. Rub snapper inside and out with garlic salt and pepper in equal amounts. Allow to stand while nuts toast in

300°F oven until browned. Melt butter in large skillet. Add onion. Saute until soft but not brown. Place salt, cucumber, cloves, sage and 1/2 cup toasted almonds in blender container. Cover. Blend on low speed 15 seconds or until cucumber and nuts are coarsely chopped. Add bread cubes to skillet with onions. Toss to mix thoroughly. Turn into large mixing bowl. Add blender contents. Toss. Moisten dressing with white wine. Toss lightly. Stuff fish. Sew up tightly. Score both sides of fish deeply in several places. Insert small pieces of raw bacon into slits. Rinse and dry blender container. Place remaining nuts in container. Cover. Blend on low speed until nuts are pulverized. Remove cap from cover. Pour in enough melted butter and white wine, mixed in equal amounts, to make a smooth paste. Pat over entire upper side of fish. Bake in well buttered, ovenprooof serving dish in 375°F oven about 1 hour or until crust is deeply browned and crisp. Baste every 10 minutes with more butter-wine mixture. Serve at once.

SAUMON AU CHAMPAGNE

4 to 6 salmon filets
1-1/2 cups champagne
1 tomato
3 to 4 sliced mushrooms

1 tsp. minced parsley
salt, pepper
1 cup (1/2 pt.) whipping cream
butter

Place salmon in buttered dish. Pour champagne over fish. Peel, seed and slice tomato. Place on top of salmon. Add mushrooms, parsley, salt and pepper. Cover closely with waxed paper. Poach fish in 350°F oven about 15 minutes or until fish flakes when tested with fork. Remove filets carefully from pan. Place on paper toweling to drain. Then place in flameproof serving dish. Keep warm. Pour poaching liquid and vegetables into blender container. Cover. Blend on high speed 30 seconds. Pour mixture into large skillet. Add cream. Boil sauce rapidly until it begins to thicken, about 10 minutes. Start adding butter 1 tablespoon at a time. Stir until melted. Continue until sauce is thick enough to spread. Coat fish with sauce. Run under hot broiler until nicely browned. Serve at once.

BAKED SALMON MOUSSE

3 tbs. butter
2 tsp. flour
salt, cayenne
1/2 tsp. dry mustard

1/3 cup milk
1-3/4 lb. salmon
3 egg yolks
2 tbs. sherry

nutmeg, anchovy paste
3 egg whites
1 cup (1/2 pt.) whipping cream
Sauce Hollandaise, page 171

Place butter, flour, salt, cayenne, dry mustard and milk in blender container. Cover. Blend on low speed 15 to 30 seconds. Pour into small saucepan. Stir over moderate heat until sauce boils. Return to blender container. Skin and bone salmon. Add salmon, egg yolks, sherry and seasonings to sauce. Cover. Blend on high speed 30 seconds or until mixture is pureed. Turn into large bowl. Beat egg whites and cream until stiff. Fold into salmon mixture. Adjust seasonings. Pour into well buttered molds. Place in pan of hot water. Press a small piece of paper against the surface of each mold to prevent over browning. Bake in 375°F oven 25 to 30 minutes or until mousse is set and tests done when probed with a foodpick. Remove from oven. Allow to rest 3 minutes. Unmold. Serve with Hollandaise Sauce.

POACHED SALMON WITH HOLLANDAISE

fresh salmon
2 cups dry white wine
water
salt, peppercorns, bay leaf
Sauce Hollandaise, page 171
paprika

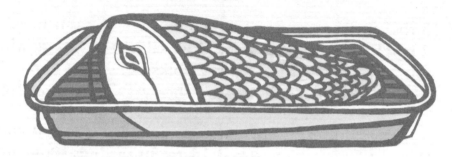

Select a piece of salmon suitable for the number of servings desired. Wrap it securely in cheese cloth. Place on rack in large pan or poacher. Add wine and enough water to cover the fish. Season with salt, peppercorns and bay leaf. Cover. Bring slowly to boil. Reduce heat. Simmer slowly 15 to 30 minutes depending on size. Lift rack from pan. Allow fish to drain. Make Hollandaise Sauce. Remove cheese cloth from fish. Roll the piece onto a serving platter. Spread sauce carefully over salmon. Dust lightly with paprika. Garnish with parsley. Serve with tiny boiled new potatoes.

64

BRANDADE OF SALT COD

1 lb. salt codfish	3/4 cup cream
1 garlic clove	3/4 cup olive oil

Soak codfish in cold water for 12 hours. Change the water often. Drain thoroughly. Break into small chunks. Place in saucepan. Cover with cold water. Bring to a boil. Drain off water. Re-cover with cold water. Bring to boil. Lower heat. Simmer 10 to 15 minutes or until fish is very tender. Drain thoroughly. Discard skin and bones. Place fish in blender container. Add garlic, 3 tablespoons cream and 3 tablespoons olive oil. Cover. Blend on high speed 15 to 30 seconds. Remove cap from cover. With blender still running on high speed, add cream and olive oil 2 tablespoons at a time until mixture is light, creamy and shiny smooth. It should not be runny. You should be able to add at least 1/2 cup each of oil and cream, and maybe even more without destroying the emulsion. Reheat the brandade gently over extremely low heat. Serve with warm white toast.

Note: Finnan Haddie may be used instead of salt codfish. Soak only 2 to 3 hours.

FILET OF SOLE GRANVILLAISE ETUVES CARVALHO

For this dish you should really have not only the filets of sole, but the carcass as well.

6 filets of sole
1/2 cup water
3/4 cup dry white wine
3 to 4 peppercorns
1 tsp. dried tarragon leaves
2 egg yolks
cayenne pepper
1/2 cup (1/4 lb.) hot, melted butter
3 ripe tomatoes, peeled and seeded.

Place the fish carcass (ask your butcher for one) in a medium-sized, lightly greased saucepan. Add water, wine, a tiny bit of salt, peppercorns and tarragon. Bring to a boil. Lower heat. Simmer 15 minutes. While court-bouillon is cooking, cut the filets in half lengthwise, so you have 12 strips. Fold strips in half crosswise with the skin inside. Lay side by side in shallow, buttered baking dish. Strain court-bouillon. Pour over filets. Cover fish closely with waxed paper. Poach 15 minutes in 350°F oven. Remove fish to absorbent paper to drain. Place on serving platter in a clock pattern. Keep warm. Strain liquid back into saucepan. Boil furiously until it has reduced to about 2 teaspoonfuls. Place this highly concentrated fish fumet in blender container. Add egg yolks and cayenne. Cover. Blend on low speed. Remove cap and pour hot melted butter directly into blades. Stop blending as soon as sauce thickens and resembles hollandaise. Coarsely chop tomatoes. Cook briskly in a small amount of hot butter until moisture has cooked away. Tomatoes should be firm, not mushy. To serve, coat filets with sauce. Make a mound of tomato puree in the middle of the clock. Sprinkle a tiny bit of tarragon on each filet. Makes 6 servings.

FILET OF SOLE GRAND DUC

6 filets of sole
juice of 1 lemon
3/4 cup dry white wine
1/2 cup water

1 bay leaf
3 to 4 peppercorns
1/2 tsp. salt
1 lb. asparagus

Wash sole in lemon juice and water. Fold filets in half, skin side in. Arrange in lightly buttered baking dish. Combine wine, water, bay leaf, peppercorns and salt. Pour over fish. Cover closely with waxed paper. Poach in 350°F oven 15 minutes. While fish is poaching, cook asparagus using the Paul Mayer Method, page 108. Cut asparagus into 1/2 inch pieces. Put butter, flour, salt, cayenne and liquid from fish in blender container. Cover. Blend on high speed 15 to 30 seconds, or until completely smooth. Pour into small saucepan. Stir over moderate heat until sauce boils. Thin to desired consistency with cream. Stir in asparagus pieces. Place fish briefly on absorbent paper. Arrange on flameproof serving dish. Pour sauce over filets. Sprinkle with grated Parmesan. Dot with butter. Run under hot broiler until surface is nicely browned. Makes 4 to 6 servings.

68

FILET OF SOLE DUGLERE

8 filets of sole   salt, cayenne pepper
3 ripe tomatoes   1/2 to 1 cup cream
2 tbs. fresh parsley   freshly grated Parmesan cheese
1/4 cup butter   butter

Poach filets following directions given in Filet of Sole Grand Duc on page 68. While fish is poaching, peel and seed tomatoes. Cut into small shreds or julienne. Chop parsley. Place butter, flour, salt and pepper in blender container. Strain poaching liquid and add. Cover. Blend on high speed 15 to 30 seconds or until mixture is smooth. Pour into small saucepan. Stir over medium heat until mixture boils and becomes quite thick. Thin to a nice consistency with cream. Be careful not to thin too much. Add tomatoes and parsley. Drain fish. Place on absorbent paper a few moments to remove excess liquid. Arrange on flameproof serving dish. Pour sauce over filets. Sprinkle with Parmesan. Dot liberally with small pieces of butter. Run under hot broiler until surface is nicely browned. Makes 8 servings.

FILET OF SOLE MARGUREY

6 filets of sole
3 to 4 mushrooms
2 tbs. butter
1/4 lb. tiny shrimp
1/2 lb. cooked mussels

2 tsp. chopped parsley
Sauce Hollandaise, page 171
2 tbs. butter
1/4 cup flour
1/2 to 1 cup cream

Poach filets following the directions given in Filet of Sole Grand Duc on page 68. While fish is poaching, slice and saute mushrooms in hot butter. Add shrimp, mussels, parsley, salt and pepper. Set aside. Prepare Hollandaise Sauce. Set aside. Place butter, flour, salt and pepper in blender container. Strain poaching liquid and add. Cover. Blend on high speed until smooth. Pour into small saucepan. Stir over moderate heat until mixture boils and becomes quite thick. Thin to a nice spreading consistency with cream. Add Hollandaise. Stir to blend. Carefully dry filets. Arrange on flameproof serving dish. Scatter shrimp-mussel mixture over filets. Pour on sauce. Run under hot broiler until bubbly and browned. Makes 6 servings.

70

TRUITE NANO

4 to 6 large trout	4 egg yolks
3/4 cup dry white wine	1/2 cup whipping cream
1/2 cup water	4 tsp. parsley
1 bay leaf	4 tsp. chives
3 to 4 peppercorns	1/4 cup raw spinach leaves
salt	

Bone trout. Lay in a lightly buttered baking dish. Combine wine, water, bay leaf, peppercorns and salt. Pour over trout. Cover closely with waxed paper. Poach in 350°F oven 15 minutes. Remove trout to serving dish. Keep warm. Strain poaching liquid. Measure 1/2 cup of liquid into small saucepan. Reduce it rapidly until it measures 2 tablespoons. Place in blender container with remaining ingredients. Cover. Blend on medium speed 30 seconds or until spinach is well chopped. Turn into small saucepan. Stir over low heat until sauce thickens and coats spoon. Spread over trout. Serve at once. Makes 4 to 6 servings.

ZUGERSEE BALCHEN MIT KRAUTERSAUCE

Balchen is a small fish found only in Lake Zug in Switzerland, but fillet of sole is equally delicious. "Krautersauce" means herb sauce not sauerkraut!

6 filets of sole	3/4 cup dry white wine
butter	2 cups (1 pt.) whipping cream
salt, freshly ground pepper	1-1/2 tsp. <u>each</u> parsley, chervil,
3/4 cup water	chives, marjoram, basil

Fold filets skin-side in. Arrange in shallow baking dish. Dot with butter. Season. Pour water and wine over filets. Cover closely with waxed paper. Poach in 350°F oven 15 minutes. Drain poaching liquid into blender container. Add remaining ingredients. Cover. Blend on medium speed about 15 seconds. Pour into large skillet. Reduce briskly until sauce starts to thicken. Adjust seasonings. Begin adding butter, 1 tablespoon at a time, until sauce has thickened enough to spread. Pat filets dry on paper toweling. Coat with sauce. Run under hot broiler until browned. Makes 6 servings.

SCAMPI FLAMBEES BELLES ALLIANCE

This creation comes from the Hotel Prinses Juliana in the Dutch town of Valkenburg, whose dining room leaves not one thing to be desired in either service or food.

2 shallots
1 carrot
1 tsp. each thyme, tarragon, parsley
1/4 cup butter
bay leaf
48 medium uncooked shrimp
1/4 cup brandy

1/4 cup Calvados
1/4 cup dry white wine
2 tbs. butter
2 tbs. flour
liquid from shrimp
1 tomato, peeled and seeded
1/2 cup cream

Finely chop shallots, carrots, thyme, tarragon and parsley. Melt butter in deep pan. Add chopped ingredients. Saute until soft. Add bay leaf and shrimp, still in their shells. Toss until they turn pink. Pour in brandy. Ignite. When flame goes out add Calvados. Ignite again. Add wine. Simmer 5 minutes. Remove shrimp from pot. Reserve liquid. Spread shrimp out for faster cooling. Shell as soon as cool enough to handle. Place butter, flour and strained shrimp liquid in blender container. Add tomato. Cover. Blend on medium speed until smooth. Pour into saucepan. Stir over moderate heat until sauce boils. Add cream. Allow to reduce until sauce is nicely thickened. Season to taste. Add shelled shrimp. Gently reheat. Serve in individual ramekins as a first course or with rice as an entree. Garnish with chopped parsley. Makes 6 to 8 servings.

CREVETTES AU BEURRE DES HERBES

A memorable meal at Les Fougeres, a superlative restaurant in Albany, New York, began with this delicious creation of Shrimp with Herb Butter.

1 lb. medium, raw shrimp	6 pitted black olives
juice of 1 lemon	small garlic clove
6 tbs. melted butter	1 tsp. parsley
1 medium onion	1 tsp. tarragon
3 to 4 anchovy filets	1 cup dry white wine

Remove shells, vein and tails from shrimp. Wash in water with lemon juice added. Drain. Place remaining ingredients in blender container. Cover. Blend on medium speed until chopped. Pour into large skillet. Cook briskly until wine is nearly gone. Add shrimp. Continue cooking until wine is completely gone and shrimp have turned pink. Toss frequently. Serve at once in small individual ramekins as a first course or over rice as an entree. Makes 4 to 6 servings.

SAVORY BAKED OYSTERS

6 shallots, cut in half
1 anchovy filet
3 walnut meats
1 small clove garlic
2 tbs. butter
6 oysters
rock salt
bacon

Place shallots, anchovy, nuts, garlic and butter in blender container. Cover. Blend on high speed 15 seconds or until well chopped. Turn into small skillet. Cook slowly until moisture has cooked away and shallots are soft. Season with a little pepper only. Loosen oysters from shell. Scrub shells. Replace oysters. Spread them sparsely with mixture. Place on a deep bed of rock salt. Bake in 475°F oven until mixture is sizzling. Place a small piece of bacon on each oyster. Run under hot broiler until bacon crisps. Serve at once. Makes 6 servings.

Poultry

Well prepared poultry dishes can be delightful and are relatively inexpensive. Chicken, particularly, lends itself to a number of methods of preparation in which the blender can be tremendously helpful.

Because of its versatility and its own good flavor, chicken has been the mainstay of the great cuisines of the world and a favorite of almost every country. It adapts easily to regional preferences such as the curries of India, the wines of France or the spices of Spain, Mexico or South America.

Second only to its need to be the freshest you can buy, is the importance of chicken being thoroughly cooked. One of the best tests I know is to place it on a white plate and then pierce the thigh with the tines of a fork. The juice which comes forth should be clear. If tinged with pink, it is not done enough.

I highly recommend the following recipes for new ways to enjoy chicken.

POULET EN CREME SAUCE

3-1/2 lb. chicken
2 onions
2 carrots
2 stalks celery
salt, peppercorns
1 bay leaf
1/4 cup butter
1/4 cup flour
1 cup milk
1 cup (1/2 pt.) whipping cream
4 egg yolks
1/4 tsp. paprika

Place trussed chicken in Dutch oven or deep kettle. Coarsely chop onions, carrots and celery. Add to pot along with salt, peppercorns and bay leaf. Barely cover chicken with water. Bring slowly to boil. Reduce heat. Simmer gently 30

minutes or until chicken is thoroughly cooked, but not overly so. (One of the best tests I know for testing chicken is to pierce the thigh with the tines of a fork. The juice should run clear. If it is tinged with pink the chicken is not done). Remove chicken from pot. When cool enough to handle remove meat from chicken. Cut in fairly large cubes. Turn up the heat under the kettle. Quickly reduce broth until it measures 1 cup. Strain out vegetables. Pour reduced broth into blender container with butter, flour, milk, whipping cream, salt and cayenne. Cover. Blend on high speed from 15 to 30 seconds, or until everything is well mixed. Pour into saucepan. Stir over moderate heat until mixture boils. Return to blender. Add egg yolks. Cover. Blend on low speed 15 seconds or until yolks have thickened the sauce. Add paprika. Blend 5 seconds. Add diced chicken to sauce. Heat gently to serving temperature. Do not allow to boil, lest it curdle. Makes 6 servings.

Note: This dish may be further enbellished by adding sauteed mushrooms, finely chopped and sauteed green pepper, and pimiento to make Chicken A La King.

POULET SAUTE NOT SO SEC

2-1/2 to 3 lb. chicken
salt, pepper
3 to 4 tbs. butter
2 finely chopped onions

1/2 cup dry white wine
1/2 lb. mushroom caps
1 tsp. each parsley, chives, tarragon
Saute Sauce, page 85

Cut chicken into serving pieces. Season with salt and pepper. Melt butter in large skillet. Add onion. Place chicken pieces on top of onions. Cook 5 minutes, turning pieces frequently. Put remaining ingredients in blender container. Cover. Blend on low speed 15 to 30 seconds, or until mushrooms are chopped. Pour mixture over chicken. Cover pan. Lower heat. Simmer gently 25 minutes. Turn pieces once halfway through cooking time. (Make sauce while chicken is cooking.) When chicken is tender, remove lid. Allow liquid to cook away until contents of skillet are merely buttery. Arrange on serving platter. Pour sauce into skillet. Stir to combine with pan juices. Pour over chicken. Garnish with paprika and sprigs of parsley.

SAUTE SAUCE

2 tbs. butter
3 tbs. flour
1 cup milk
1/2 cup whipping cream
salt, cayenne pepper to taste
2 egg yolks
1/8 tsp. paprika

Place butter, flour, milk, cream, salt and cayenne in blender container. Cover. Blend on high speed 15 to 30 seconds. Pour into saucepan. Stir over moderate heat until mixture boils. Return to blender. Add egg yolks. Cover. Blend on low speed 10 seconds, or until yolks thicken sauce. Add paprika. Stop blender. Taste for seasoning. Correct if necessary. Use sauce as directed.

CHICKEN BREASTS EN PAPILLOTE

6 chicken breast halves
1 egg white
2 tbs. whipping cream
salt, pepper
2 truffles
2 to 3 oz. foie gras
6 tbs. butter
parchment paper
1/2 cup port wine
1/2 cup chicken broth
butter

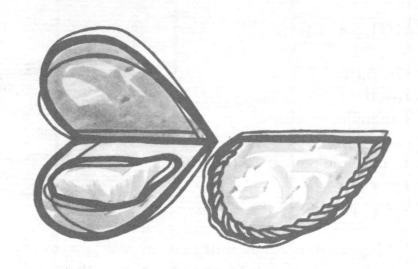

Bone the breasts. Remove the small filet from each piece. Run these little pieces of breast through the fine blade of a meat grinder. Place ground meat in blender container with egg white and 2 tablespoons cream. Cover. Blend thoroughly. Add more cream, a little at a time, forcing the mixture into the blades until it is smooth and shiny, but not fluid. It must hold its shape. Add salt and pepper, 1 chopped truffle and foie gras to blender. Cover. Run on medium speed until well mixed, about 30 seconds. Make a lengthwise slit in each piece of breast by running the knife in between the top and bottom of the breast to create a pocket. Stuff with filling. Melt butter in skillet. Cook breasts slowly in foaming butter for about 15 minutes. Turn frequently to prevent them from browning. While breasts are cooking, cut 6 heart-shaped pieces of parchment large enough to cover breasts when folded in half. Fold hearts in half lengthwise. Oil paper well on both sides. Place a piece of breast on one half of each heart. Close the "papillote." Seal by folding over the edges like a hem. Place on baking sheets. Bake in 350°F oven 12 minutes. Cut remaining truffle in julienne strips. Add to butter in skillet. Stir in port and broth. Bring to a boil. Thicken by adding butter a little at a time until desired consistency is reached. Serve breasts still wrapped. Pass sauce separately. Makes 6 servings.

BALLOTINE OF CHICKEN A LA REGENCE

A truly magnificent version of hot Chicken Galatin. A bit of work to be sure, but dear to the heart of the hostess, it can be prepared in advance and worth the effort.

1 large broiler-fryer	bouquet garni*, page 87
veal bones	Farce a Quenelles a la Panade, page 88
2 onions	2 or 3 chopped truffles
4 whole cloves	1/2 lb. piece cooked tongue
2 carrots, sliced	mushroom caps
1 clove garlic	artichoke bottoms
2 tsp. salt	ripe green olives
8 peppercorns	Sauce Supreme Gourmet, page 169

Carefully bone chicken. Put chicken bones, veal bones, onions stuck with cloves, carrots, garlic, salt, peppercorns and bouquet garni in pot with 2-1/2 quarts water. Bring to a boil. Reduce heat and simmer slowly until needed. Spread boned chicken with a layer of Farce Quenelles a la Panade. Sprinkle with truffles. Cut tongue in pieces 4 inches by 1 inch thick. Lay lengthwise on top of truffles. Cover tongue with another layer of the farce. Roll chicken lengthwise into a firm roll. Sew it tightly. Roll in waxed paper, then in a large kitchen towel. Tie cloth tightly at both ends and at intervals between so the ballotine will hold its shape while cooking. Bring liquid to boiling again. Place ballotine in pan. As soon as broth begins to boil again, reduce heat. Simmer ballotine 60 minutes so the center farce will be thoroughly cooked. Remove from stock. Unwrap. Allow to stand 5 minutes. Untie. Cut into 8 thick slices using a sharp knife. Overlap slices on warmed platter. Garnish with mushroom caps, artichoke bottoms and olives which have all been tossed in hot butter to cook slightly. Coat with Sauce Supreme Gourmet. Pass extra sauce.

*Bouquet garni—Tie 3 sprigs of parsley, 1 bay leaf and a pinch of thyme together in a small piece of cheesecloth.

FARCE A QUENELLAS A LA PANADE

1/2 cup flour	6 tbs. milk
4 egg yolks	2/3 cup ground lean veal
1/2 cup melted butter	2 eggs
salt, pepper, nutmeg	2 tbs. whipping cream

Measure flour, 2 egg yolks, 5 tablespoons butter, salt, pepper, nutmeg and milk into blender container. Cover. Blend on high speed 15 to 30 seconds. Pour mixture into small saucepan. Gradually bring to boiling over low heat. Continue cooking, stirring vigorously, 5 to 6 minutes. Spread mixture on lightly buttered plate. Chill. Place chilled panade in blender container with ground veal, remaining butter and egg yolks, whole eggs and whipping cream. Cover. Blend on high speed 1 minute. Force through a fine sieve. Use as directed in Ballotine of Chicken a la Regence, page 86.

SUPREMA POLLO FARCITA

6 chicken breast halves	1/4 cup butter
3 small zucchini	2 tbs. olive oil
1/4 lb. Fontina cheese	3 tbs. Marsala wine
1/4 lb. Parmesan cheese	2 tbs. cream

Bone breasts. Place between two sheets of waxed paper. Pound gently until very thin. (Avoid tearing the flesh.) Cut zucchini and cheese into chunks. Put into blender container. Cover. Blend on low speed 15 to 30 seconds or until zucchini is chopped and mixed with cheese. Place a spoonful of this mixture in the center of each piece of breast. Fold breast over filling, making tightly closed packages. Tie each with string. Dust lightly with flour. Melt butter in skillet. Cook breasts slowly in hot butter about 15 to 20 minutes. Turn frequently so cheese will melt and zucchini will be cooked. When done, remove to a serving dish. Add olive oil, Marsala and cream to the skillet. Cook until sauce thickens. Pour sauce over chicken. Run under the broiler to brown the sauce. Makes 6 servings.

Meat

As meats are not normally put into the blender, this chapter is necessarily limited to those meat recipes which are made easier through the use of a blender.

Many of the recipes in this book were collected during my travels in Europe where meat has always been expensive. In some of the world's most elegant recipes, the amount of meat used is relatively small. It is the sauce, or stuffing or other additions which make these dishes unusual and delicious. Great care is given to their preparation and a little meat is made to go a long way. Most frequently it is braised, after being browned in butter, with other ingredients chosen to bring out its best flavor. Even when steak or rare roast beef is served, it is almost always accompanied by a special sauce. Our hastily broiled, unadorned beef is considered by Europeans as slightly barbaric or, at best, a sign of our lack of respect for it.

I hope my recipes will be welcomed additions to your repertoire of favorites.

SWEDISH MEATBALLS IN SOUR CREAM SAUCE

3/4 lb. ground round
3/4 lb. ground lean veal
2 cups bread cubes
milk
1 medium onion, quartered
1/4 cup melted butter

3 eggs
salt & pepper, to taste
2 tsp. nutmeg
2 tsp. paprika
1 tsp. dry mustard
1 tsp. dried dill weed

Place meat in large mixing bowl. Soak bread cubes in a small amount of milk. Squeeze bread almost dry. Crumble into bowl with meat. Put onion pieces and melted butter into blender container. Cover. Run blender on low speed about 20 seconds, or until onion is chopped. Turn into small skillet. Saute until onion begins to brown. Add to meat. Break eggs into blender container. Add salt, pepper, nutmeg, paprika, dry mustard and dill weed. Cover. Run blender on highest speed 15 to 30 seconds, or until thoroughly blended. Add to meat. Work mixture together with hands. Shape meat into small balls.

SOUR CREAM SAUCE

3 tbs. butter
1 clove garlic, minced
2 tsp. Bovril
2 tsp. tomato paste
1/4 cup flour
1 cup water
2 cups (1 pt.) sour cream (room temperature)
1 tbs. dried dill weed

Melt butter in large skillet. Brown meatballs quickly, but thoroughly. Remove from pan. Add garlic to drippings. Cook slowly, 2 minutes. Measure Bovril, tomato paste, flour and water in blender container. Cover. Run machine on high speed 15 seconds or until well mixed. Add to garlic. Stir over medium heat until sauce thickens and boils. Remove from heat. Carefully stir in sour cream and dill weed. Add meatballs to sauce. Simmer gently 5 to 7 minutes before serving. Makes 6 servings.

 PAUL'S MEAT LOAF

1-1/2 lbs. ground chuck or round steak
4 slices firm white bread
milk
salt, black pepper

1 small onion, cut into pieces
3 tbs. chili sauce
3 to 5 tbs. mayonnaise

Crumble meat into mixing bowl. Soak bread in milk. Squeeze dry. Put into blender container. Add remaining ingredients. Cover. Blend on low speed 15 to 30 seconds or until everything is chopped and well mixed. Add to meat. Mix thoroughly with hands. Correct seasoning. Pack into well-greased loaf pan. Spread entire surface with more chili sauce. Bake in 350°F oven 30 to 45 minutes. Do not overcook or meat loaf will become dry. Remove from oven. Allow to rest at least 5 minutes before removing from pan. Slice. Serve as is, or with a tomato sauce of your choice. Cool, then wrap in foil if it is to be served cold. Chill for easier slicing.

BARBECUED SPARERIBS

3 lbs. meaty spareribs
1 tbs. butter or bacon fat
1/2 small onion
1/2 cup water
2 tbs. tarragon vinegar
1 tbs. Worcestershire sauce

1/4 cup lemon juice
1 tbs. light brown sugar
1 bottle (12 oz.) chili sauce
1/2 tsp. salt
1/4 tsp. paprika

Cut spareribs into serving-sized pieces. When ready to prepare, put remaining ingredients in blender container. Cover. Blend on low speed 15 to 30 seconds, or until onion is chopped and blended with other ingredients. Pour mixture into a large skillet. Simmer over low heat 20 minutes. While sauce is simmering, place ribs in a large baking pan. Cover with foil. Bake in 500°F oven 15 minutes. Lower heat to 350°F. Pour sauce over ribs. Continue baking about one hour, or until sauce dries out somewhat and meat is soft to the point of leaving the bones. Baste every 10 minutes, or so, with pan drippings. Turn pieces once during baking.

VEAL OSCAR

18 asparagus spears, cooked
12 whole crab legs
1-1/2 lbs. thin veal
seasoned flour
butter
1 clove garlic
1/2 tsp. Bovril
1/2 tsp. tomato paste
1 tbs. potato starch
1/2 cup Madeira or Marsala wine
1 cup stock
2 tsp. red current jelly
bay leaf
Sauce Bearnaise, page 172

Use 3 asparagus spears and 2 crab legs per serving. Cut veal in 2 inch pieces.

Place between sheets of waxed paper. Pound until very thin. Dust lightly with seasoned flour. Melt butter in large skillet. Quickly brown meat. Pour in brandy. Ignite. When flame goes out, remove meat from pan. Put garlic through press into pan. Saute slowly one minute. Put Bovril, tomato paste, potato starch, wine and stock in blender container. Cover. Blend on high speed until well mixed. Add to frying pan with garlic. Stir over moderate heat until sauce thickens and boils. Add jelly and bay leaf. Return veal to pan. Simmer gently, uncovered, 20 minutes. Prepare Bearnaise Sauce during this time. When ready to serve, arrange veal on warm serving dish. Top with sauce. Lay asparagus on top of sauce. Place crab legs on asparagus. Cover with Bearnaise Sauce. Run dish quickly under broiler to brown surface. Serve at once. Makes 6 servings.

SCHNITZEL ROYAL

4 veal cutlets
1 egg
seasoned flour
butter
4 thin slices smoked ham
12 cooked asparagus spears
Sauce Gruyere, page 99

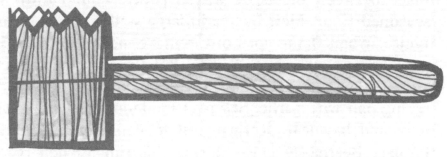

Place cutlets between two sheets of waxed paper. Pound with a heavy mallet. Beat egg with one teaspoon water. Dip cutlets into flour. Shake off excess. Dip in beaten egg, then in flour again. Heat butter in large skillet until foaming. Slowly brown cutlets on both sides. Remove from pan to a flameproof platter. Cover each cutlet with a ham slice. Lay asparagus spears on ham. Top with Sauce Gruyere. Run platter under broiler until nicely browned. Serve at once.

SAUCE GRUYERE

2 tbs. butter
3 tbs. flour
salt, cayenne pepper, to taste
pinch dry mustard
3/4 cup milk
1/2 cup (2 oz.) Gruyere cheese

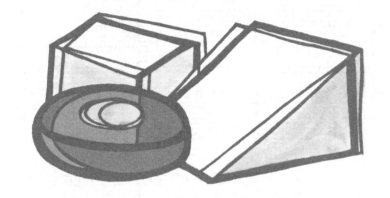

Put all ingredients in blender container. Blend on high speed 15 to 30 seconds or until cheese is grated. Pour into saucepan. Stir over moderate heat until sauce thickens and boils. Use as directed.

BLANQUETTE DE VEAU

2 lbs. boneless veal
1 sliced onion
1 sliced carrot
2 stalks celery
1 bay leaf
3 to 4 peppercorns

1 tsp. salt
12 white boiling onions
1/2 lb. mushrooms
butter
Sauce Veloute, page 101

Cut veal into one inch cubes. Place in kettle. Cover with cold water. Bring slowly to boil. As soon as it has boiled, discard water. Rinse meat well in cold water. Clean the pot. Put meat back in pot. Add onion, carrot, celery, bay leaf, peppercorns and salt. Bring to boil again. Simmer gently until meat is tender, about one hour. While meat is cooking, boil onions until tender. Do not over cook. Cut mushrooms into quarters. Saute in very hot butter until browned. Drain onions. Add to mushrooms. When veal is done, drain it. Reserve two cups cooking liquid. Combine veal with onions and mushrooms. Pour sauce over meat and vegetables. Garnish with paprika and parsley. Serve immediatly.

100

SAUCE VELOUTE

5 tbs. butter
6 tbs. flour
salt, cayenne pepper to taste
2 cups reserved stock
4 tsp. butter
1/4 cup cream
2 egg yolks
1 tsp. lemon juice

Place butter, flour, salt, cayenne and stock in blender container. Cover. Run on high speed 15 to 30 seconds, or until smooth. Turn out into a deep saucepan. Stir over moderate heat until mixture thickens and boils. Remove from heat. Return to blender container. Add butter, cream, egg yolks and lemon juice. Cover. Blend on low speed until well mixed and the sauce has thickened slightly. Use as directed. Makes 4 to 6 servings.

VEAL CORDON BLEU

6 slices veal
6 slices boiled ham
6 slices Gruyere cheese
1 egg
1 tsp. water
flour
fine dry bread crumbs
hot deep fat (380°F)
Tomato Sauce, page 176

Trim veal. Place between pieces of waxed paper. Pound with a mallet until very thin. Beat egg and water together. Remove top sheet of waxed paper. Paint each veal slice with egg. Place ham on one half of each veal slice. Lay cheese on top of ham. Fold veal over cheese to make a sealed package. Dip in flour, then beaten egg, then crumbs. Fry in hot fat until deeply browned and crisp. Drain on absorbent paper. Serve with Tomato Sauce. Makes 6 servings.

SWEETBREADS

Sweetbreads always require preliminary preparation. Bear this in mind, and give yourself plenty of starting time before making any kind of a dish involving them. This preparation can be completed successfully the night before and the sweetbreads left pressing between two plates until time to use them.

sweetbreads   juice of 1 lemon

Put sweetbreads in pan. Cover with water. Add lemon juice. Bring slowly to boiling. Reduce heat. Simmer gently 5 minutes. Drain. Plunge into a bowl of iced water. Skin carefully. Place on plate. Set a second plate on top of sweetbreads. Press down with a 2 pound weight. (I keep a foil covered brick for just such purposes). Refrigerate at least one hour or overnight, if desired. When ready to use, remove weight and dry sweetbreads carefully on paper toweling. Proceed as directed in recipe.

Often served in a cream sauce, sweetbreads lack eye appeal. Not so when simmered in a wine sauce and served on a bed of pureed peas as in the next recipe.

BRAISED SWEETBREADS WITH PUREED PEAS

4 to 5 small pairs sweetbreads
seasoned flour
butter
2 tbs. brandy
1 clove garlic
1 tbs. finely chopped onion
1/2 tsp. tomato paste
1 tsp. Bovril

1 tbs. potato flour
1/2 cup dry white wine
1 cup stock
2 tbs. sherry
1 bay leaf, salt, pepper
1 tsp. red current jelly
Pureed Peas, page 105

Prepare sweetbreads for cooking as directed on page 103. Dust lightly with flour. Heat butter until foaming. Slowly brown sweetbreads on both sides. Add brandy. Ignite. Remove sweetbreads from pan. Put garlic through press into pan. Add onion. Cook slowly one minute. Measure tomato paste, Bovril, potato flour, wine, stock and sherry into blender container. Cover. Blend on high speed 15 to 20 seconds. Pour into pan with garlic and onion. Cook over moderate heat, stirring constantly, until sauce thickens and boils. Add bay leaf, salt, pepper and jelly. Put sweetbreads back into pan with sauce. Simmer gently no longer than 20 minutes. Turn once. While sweetbreads are simmering, prepare Pureed Peas. When ready to serve, put Pureed Peas in serving dish. Arrange sweetbreads on top of peas. Spoon hot sauce, which has been strained to remove garlic and onion pieces, over sweetbreads. Garnish with parsley. Serve at once.

PUREED PEAS

2 pkg. (10 oz. ea.) frozen peas	2 tbs. flour
2 tbs. butter	1/4 cup cream

Cook peas just until barely done. Force through food mill to remove skins. Put puree into blender container. Add remaining ingredients. Cover. Blend on high speed 15 seconds. Pour into small saucepan. Stir over moderate heat until mixture thickens and boils. Lower heat. Continue stirring two minutes longer. Use as directed.

Vegetables

Fresh vegetables, carefully prepared, are one of the true pleasures of the table. Not only do they add flavor and texture to a meal, but beautiful color as well. It is extremely important to cook vegetables in such a way as to preserve their bright color and firm texture. Nothing destroys vegetables so completely as overcooking. My special method for cooking fresh green vegetables is given on the next page.

The recipes which I have chosen to present here are a little different, and dressed up a bit, since my students are always requesting new ways of preparing vegetables, especially for entertaining. These particular dishes are designed to be served with simply prepared entrees, such as roasts, chops or steaks. When serving richly sauced entrees, be sure to keep the vegetables as simple and unassuming as possible. In almost every case, these recipes can be prepared in advance with only a few minutes cooking time needed just before serving.

107

PAUL'S METHOD FOR COOKING GREEN VEGETABLES

First off, let us consider a way of cooking green vegetables which is guaranteed to retain their color, texture and flavor. This method, if followed exactly, will yield brilliant, delicious peas, green beans, brussels sprouts, asparagus and broccoli. It does not apply to root vegetables, eggplant, artichokes or spinach. Don't ask me why it works, but it works! I think it's because boiling water is poured into a hot pan so it boils immediately and never stops during the entire cooking process. If vegetables are dropped into boiling water, or if boiling water is poured over them, the water stops boiling immediately. It takes a while for it to return to a full boil, during which time the vegetables just soak instead of cooking.

Have a tea kettle full of rapidly boiling water. In another pot, with a lid, put a large handful of sugar and 1 teaspoon salt. Place over high heat until sugar just begins to caramelize. Place prepared vegetables in pot, and with the heat still at the highest point, pour in the boiling water. Clap on the lid and boil furiously for 7 minutes—not 8, or 6, or 5-1/2, or 9—but 7 minutes. Quickly drain the vegetables. Rinse briefly with cold water to stop the cooking. (The vegetable will stay hot!) Drain and season with salt, pepper and a little melted butter.

ASPERGES AU SAUCE CHANTILLY

4 egg yolks
1/4 cup lemon juice
salt, cayenne pepper
1 cup (1/2 lb.) butter, melted
1 cup (1/2 pt.) whipping cream
asparagus spears for 6 servings
freshly grated Parmesan cheese

Place egg yolks, lemon juice, salt and cayenne in blender container. Cover. Blend on low speed 10 seconds. Remove cap from cover. Add melted butter in a slow, steady stream. Blend only until all butter has been added. Pour sauce into bowl. Whip cream until stiff. Carefully fold into sauce. Spoon over asparagus spears which have been cooked using the Paul Mayer Method, page 108. Drain well. Arrange on a flameproof platter. Spoon sauce over asparagus. Sprinkle lightly with Parmesan. Run under broiler until browned. Serve at once. Makes 6 servings.

ASPERGES NEAPOLITAINE

1 lb. asparagus spears
3 tbs. butter
2 celery stalks
1 small onion
small piece of Parmesan cheese
1 tbs. fresh bread
1 can (8 oz.) Italian-style tomatoes
salt, freshly ground pepper
pinch sugar, thyme, oregano

Wash asparagus tips well. Dry thoroughly. Melt butter in an ovenproof dish. Lay asparagus in even rows in dish. Trim celery and peel with potato peeler to remove strings. Place celery, onion, Parmesan, bread, well-drained tomatoes (no juice) and seasonings in blender container. Cover. Blend on high speed 15 seconds or until cheese is grated. Spread mixture over asparagus. Bake in 375°F oven 35 to 40 minutes.

FONDS DU ARTICHAUT FAVORITE

1 jar (12 oz.) artichoke bottoms	2 tbs. butter	salt, cayenne pepper
1/2 cup artichoke liquid	1/4 cup flour	2 egg yolks
butter	1/2 cup bean liquid	1 tsp. lemon juice
1 lb. string beans	3/4 cup whipping cream	Gruyere cheese

Drain artichokes well. Reserve liquid. Saute artichoke bottoms in hot foaming butter until nicely browned. Arrange in flameproof serving dish. Run beans through French slicer (or cut by hand). Cut into 2-1/2 inch lengths. Cook, using the Paul Mayer Method, page 108. Drain beans. Reserve 1/2 cup liquid. Place butter, flour, vegetable juices, 1/2 cup cream, salt and pepper in blender container. Cover. Blend on high speed 30 seconds, or until well mixed. Pour into saucepan. Stir over medium heat until mixture boils Place egg yolks, lemon juice and the remaining 1/4 cup cream in blender container. Cover. Blend on low speed. Remove cover. Pour the very hot sauce directly into running blender. Combine sauce with beans. Spoon over artichoke hearts. Sprinkle entire surface with cheese. Place under broiler until cheese melts and is browned. Makes 6 servings.

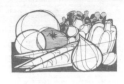

FAGIOLINI ET POMADORO (String Beans & Tomatoes)

4 ripe tomatoes
3 tbs. olive oil
1 large onion, cut in chunks
1 large garlic clove
1 tsp. crushed basil
2 lbs. green beans, trimmed

Remove skins from tomatoes by holding them in boiling water 10 seconds. Place under cold running water immediately to stop further cooking. Cut away hard centers and remove seeds. Put tomatoes, olive oil, onion chunks, garlic, sugar and basil in blender container. Cover. Blend on high speed only long enough to chop vegetables, about 15 seconds. Pour into large skillet. Reduce juices rapidly over medium-high heat until mixture is fairly thick. Cook beans using the Paul Mayer Method, page 108. Drain thoroughly. Combine with tomato mixture. Reheat only as long as necessary. Overcooking will destroy the bright green color of the beans. Makes 6 servings.

112

CELERIAC AU GRATIN

3 lbs. celery root
6 tbs. butter
6 tbs. flour
salt, cayenne pepper

1 cup (1/2 pt.) whipping cream
1/2 cup grated Parmesan cheese
pinch dry mustard
fresh, buttered bread crumbs

Peel and dice celery root. Keep in water, with a little lemon juice or vinegar added, until ready to cook. Drain. Barely cover with fresh water. Add a little salt. Bring slowly to boil. Cook until barely tender, about 10 minutes. Drain well. Strain liquid. Reserve 1-1/2 cups. Place butter, flour, salt, cayenne, cream and reserved liquid in blender container. Cover. Blend on high speed 20 seconds. Pour into saucepan. Stir over moderate heat until mixture thickens and boils. Add Parmesan and mustard. Allow to boil, stirring constantly, 2 minutes. Remove from heat. Add celery root. Mix well. Pour into large, flat casserole. Cover with a heavy layer of buttered bread crumbs. Dust with Parmesan. Bake in 350°F oven 30 minutes, or until crumbs are browned and sauce bubbly. Makes 6 servings.

113

EGGPLANT DU PAYS PROVENCALE

2 medium-sized eggplants
butter
2 lbs. tomatoes
3 tbs. olive oil
2 cloves garlic
1 stalk celery, chopped
1 tbs. parsley
1 coarsely chopped carrot
1 onion, cut into chunks
salt, pepper, basil
Gruyere cheese

Wash and dry eggplants. Do not peel. Cut into strips 4 to 5 inches long, 2 inches wide and about 1/2 inch thick. Dredge in flour. Shake off excess flour. Fry strips gently in foaming butter, until nicely browned. Peel, seed and quarter tomatoes. Place in blender container with olive oil, garlic, celery, parsley, carrot

114

and onion. Cover. Blend 20 seconds. Season highly. Pour into large skillet. Cook over medium heat until sauce reduces to a nicely thickened consistency. Remove from heat. Place a layer of eggplant strips in the bottom of a shallow baking dish. Spread some of sauce over strips. Top with a layer of grated Gruyere. Repeat in same order until dish is filled. End with cheese on top. Bake in 400°F oven 20 to 30 minutes, or until dish is sizzling and cheese is melted and golden brown. Allow to rest 5 minutes, to re-absorb oil, before serving. Makes 6 servings.

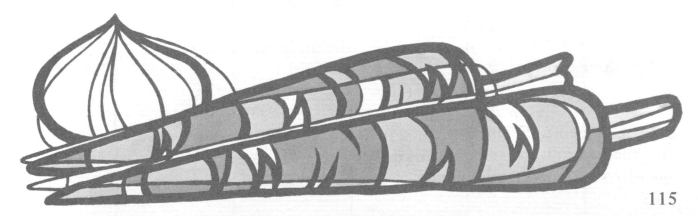

EGGPLANT CANNELONI

This is one of the greatest vegetable dishes I know. All I can say is WOW!

1 cup grated Mozzarella cheese
1/2 cup grated Parmesan cheese
1 tbs. finely chopped parsley
1 tbs. finely chopped prosciutto
1/3 cup ricotta cheese
2 eggs
salt, freshly ground pepper
1 egg white, stiffly beaten
2 tbs. flour

1/2 tsp. baking powder
1/8 tsp. salt
1/3 cup milk
1 tbs. oil
2 slender eggplants
1/4 cup olive oil
2 tbs. butter
Tomato Sauce, page 176

Combine Mozzarella, Parmesan, parsley, prosciutto, ricotta, 1 egg, salt and pepper. Blend until smooth. Fold in egg white thoroughly. Spread mixture on a flat plate. Chill. Place flour, baking powder, salt, egg, milk and cooking oil in blender container. Cover. Blend on high speed 10 to 15 seconds. Pour batter into

116

a flat pan. Peel eggplants. Cut in half lengthwise. Starting from cut surfaces, shave three thin slices from each of four pieces, yielding 12 thin, wide pieces. Dredge in flour, Shake off excess. Heat olive oil and butter together. Dip slices in batter. Saute in hot fat. Drain on paper towels. Cut chilled filling into 12 pieces. Shape into rolls. Place a roll at the broad end of each eggplant slice. Roll slices around filling. Arrange seam side down on a lightly-buttered, flameproof serving dish. Cover with Tomato Sauce. Bake in 425°F oven 10 to 15 minutes or until cheese is melted and sauce is sizzling. Garnish with chopped parsley. Makes 10 to 12 servings.

MUSHROOMS WITH GARLIC AND HERBS

1/2 cup (1/4 lb.) butter
4 finely minced shallots
1-1/2 lbs. small, whole mushrooms
salt and pepper
4 oz. Cognac
3 peeled garlic cloves

1 tbs. parsley
1/2 tsp. <u>each</u> turmeric, cumin, coriander,
   ginger, pepper
1 tsp. each rosemary, thyme, basil
3 cups whipping cream
butter

    Melt butter in skillet. Add shallots and mushrooms. Saute 2 minutes. Season. Pour in Cognac. Ignite. Put garlic, parsley, turmeric, cumin, coriander, ginger and pepper in blender container. Cover. Blend on highest speed until thoroughly minced and mixed. Add rosemary, thyme, basil and whipping cream. Cover. Blend until pulverized and mixed. Pour mixture over mushrooms. Continue cooking fairly rapidly until sauce begins to thicken. Add extra butter, one tablespoon at a time, until mixture thickens further, and does not follow the spoon when stirred across the bottom of the pan. Serve in individual ramekins. Sprinkle with finely chopped parsley. Makes 6 servings.

118

QUICHE DE POIS

1/2 cup (1/4 lb.) firm butter
2 oz. Velveeta cheese
3/4 cup flour
1 pkg. (10 oz.) frozen peas

1 cup (1/2 pt.) whipping cream
4 eggs yolks
salt, cayenne, nutmeg

Blend butter, cheese and flour together. Form into ball. Roll out on pastry cloth. Fit pastry into 8-inch layer cake pan. Rinse peas under running hot water until loosened from block. Drain on paper towels. Fill pastry with peas. Place cream, egg yolks and seasonings in blender container. Cover. Blend on highest speed 15 seconds or until yolks are well mixed with cream. Pour mixture over peas. Bake in 375°F oven 45 to 50 minutes or until top is deeply browned and custard tests done when knife inserted in center comes out clean. Remove from oven. Allow to stand 2 minutes. Invert pan onto a plate. Remove pan. Reinvert onto another plate immediately to have tart free standing and upright. Makes 4 to 6 servings.

KARTOFFEL PFANNKUCHEN (Potato Pancakes)

6 large potatoes*   1 small onion, cut in chunks
1-1/2 tbs. flour   2 whole eggs
1/4 tsp. baking powder   lard
1-1/4 tsp. salt

Peel potatoes, cut into pieces. Place a few at a time in blender container. Cover. Blend on moderate speed until all potatoes have been grated (Do not worry if they darken, just work as quickly as you can and everything will be okay.) Place grated potatoes in a large strainer or colander. Stir and press them with a large spoon until the moisture has been drained away. Return drained potatoes (there will be about 2 cups) to blender container. Add remaining ingredients. Cover. Blend on moderate speed until everything is well mixed. Pour mixture into bowl. Fry by spoonfuls in smoking lard, 1/2 inch deep, until crisp on both sides. Drain pancakes. Serve at once.

*preferably not Idahoes.

SPINACH RING

5 bunches fresh spinach	1/4 cup flour
4 eggs	1-1/2 cups milk
2 egg yolks	salt, pepper, nutmeg
1/4 cup butter	5 cup ring mold

Wash spinach several times. Steam, without adding water, just until wilted. Drain and cool. Squeeze spinach dry with hands. Grind or cut into very small pieces. Beat eggs and yolks together. Add spinach. Mix well. Put remaining ingredients into blender container. Cover. Blend on medium speed 15 to 20 seconds, or until smooth. Pour into saucepan. Stir over moderate heat until mixture boils. Add to spinach. Correct seasonings. Spoon into heavily buttered mold. Cover with a circle of buttered waxed paper. Place mold in large pan. Surround with hot water. Bake in 350°F oven 30 minutes, or until knife inserted into center comes out clean. Remove from oven. Lift from water. Allow to stand 5 minutes before unmolding. Fill center with sauteed mushrooms, glazed carrots or as desired. Makes 6 to 8 servings.

SPINACH BARNET

3 bunches fresh spinach
3 tbs. butter
2 onions
1/4 cup flour
1 tsp. Bovril
3/4 cup strong beef broth
salt, pepper

Wash spinach well. Cook just until tender. Squeeze it as dry as possible with hands. Chop coarsely. Remove heavy stems. Place in blender container with remaining ingredients. Cover. Blend on medium speed about 1 minute or until onion and spinach are chopped and ingredients are mixed. Turn mixture into heavy skillet. Stir over moderate heat until mixture thickens and boils, and is the consistency of heavy creamed spinach. Serve as is or use in the recipes that follow. Makes 6 servings.

MUSHROOMS STUFFED WITH SPINACH

24 giant mushrooms
butter
Spinach Barnet, page 123
Swiss cheese
Parmesan cheese

Remove stems from mushrooms. Save for another use. Clean mushrooms by brushing with a damp paper towel. Saute quickly in very hot butter. Do not overcook. Place mushrooms in baking dish, stem side up. Fill hollows with Spinach Barnet. Grate Swiss cheese in blender. Combine with Parmesan. Sprinkle over filled mushrooms. Bake in 425°F oven until cheese melts and tops are browned and crusty. Makes 12 servings.

STUFFED SUMMER SQUASH

summer squash
2 tbs. butter
Spinach Barnet, page 123
freshly grated Parmesan cheese

Remove stems from as many squash as desired. Hollow out each one with a small spoon, leaving a fairly thick inner wall. Melt butter in large skillet. Place squash in skillet. Cover. Cook slowly until nicely browned and tender, about 15 minutes. Turn once during cooking. Remove from skillet. Invert hollow side down to drain. Turn upright. Fill with Spinach Barnet. Place filled squash on lightly greased cookie sheet. Sprinkle with Parmesan cheese. Bake in 425°F oven until heated through and cheese is browned and crusty. Makes 6 servings.

DUTCH CURRIED KOOL SLA

We sometimes think of Dutch cooking as being the same as German. It is true that the Dutch make hearty soups and roasts, yet there is a vast influence in the Netherlands derived from Dutch colonization in the tropical climates of Indonesia. Some of their dishes are very hot, which I do not care for. Yet, mild curries are delightful. This one combines the sharp flavor of curry with another flavor, which many consider overwhelming, to yield a vegetable that is bland, interesting, subtle and absolutely great with ham!

4 lb. cabbage
1 large bay leaf
3 whole cloves
1 peeled garlic
2 tsp. Bovril or BV
2 cups hot water
pepper, to taste
3 tbs. grated onion

1 cup reserved cooking liquid
1/4 cup butter
1 tbs. curry powder
6 tbs. flour
1 cup milk
salt, cayenne pepper
1/2 cup grated Edam or Gouda cheese

126

Remove outside leaves from cabbage. Finely shred the rest. Place in colander. Quickly rinse with warm water. Put in large kettle. Make bouquet garni by tying bay leaf, cloves and garlic in cheese cloth. Bury in cabbage. Dissolve meat extract in hot water. Pour over cabbage. Add pepper and onion. Cook 10 minutes or until tender. Reserve 1 cup of the cooking liquid. Drain cabbage well. Discard bouquet garni. Place reserved liquid, butter, flour, curry, milk, salt and pepper in blender container. Cover. Blend on high speed 15 to 30 seconds or until smooth. Pour into large pan. Stir over moderate heat until mixture boils. Add cabbage to boiling sauce. Stir until well mixed. Pour into buttered casserole. Sprinkle with grated cheese. Bake in 425°F oven until bubbly and browned, about 15 minutes. Makes 6 to 8 servings.

Salads

Think of green salad as a hyphen. It connects the entree with the dessert and was designed as a palate cleanser. It was never meant to be served at the beginning of a meal! There are so many atrocities committed in the name of "salad" that when one finally does have a great one, it's like finding a pearl in an oyster. The best I ever ate was served at a French inn called Auberge des Templiers, about 75 miles from Paris. It was so delicious I had to know the secret. Mild, yet piquant, it was obiviously not made with olive oil. Presistent questioning elicited the fact that the oil was "huile de berry." It was only out of complete exasperation at my prying that the maitre d'hotel finally brought out a "berry," and I discovered it was nothing more than a walnut! The delicious salad was made with walnut oil and the blandest of white wine vinegar. Walnut oil is available in health food stores and I heartily recommend it.

JUST RIGHT FRENCH DRESSING

So-called "French" dressing can be made most successfully in the blender, but I hesitate to give you anything like a definite recipe for it, since its preparation depends so very much upon individual tastes. However, I can suggest a method by which you can arrive at just the right proportion of oil to vinegar to please you.

Start with equal amounts of oil and vinegar in the blender container. Season to your liking with salt, paprika and dry mustard. Cover container. Blend on low speed about 5 seconds. Taste the result. It will be far too tart! Start adding oil 2 tablespoons at a time. Blend. Taste. Continue in this fashion until you have a combination that pleases you. Measure the amount of dressing you have. If you started with 1/2 cup of oil and 1/2 cup of vinegar, and after adding and tasting, the final amount measures 1-1/2 cups you will have added another 1/2 cup of oil. The ratio of oil to vinegar that pleases you is 2 to 1. Make a note of this ratio. Always make your dressings to that measurement and it will be perfect every time.

ASPERGES VINAIGRETTE

2 lbs. asparagus
1 cup olive oil
1/2 cup tarragon vinegar
salt, pepper
pinch dry mustard, paprika
2 to 3 tbs. each capers, chives
2 to 3 tbs. Kosher-style dill pickle pieces

Cook asparagus according to the Paul Mayer Method on page 108. Drain and dry. Chill. Remove seeds from pickles. Combine with remaining ingredients in blender container. Cover. Blend on low speed 5 seconds only. To serve, arrange chilled asparagus on salad plates. Spoon dressing over asparagus. Serve well chilled. Makes 6 to 8 servings.

SALAD DE BOEUF

Start this salad the day before.

1 lb. chuck or round steak
1 onion
2 to 3 stalks celery
1 carrot
2 to 3 whole peppercorns
1/4 cup green pepper, cut juliene

2 tbs. thinly sliced gherkins
1 tbs. chopped onion
1 tbs. chopped parsley
1/4 cup peeled, seeded, diced tomatoes
Sauce Vinaigrette, page 133

Remove fat from beef. Coarsely chop celery and carrot. Place in kettle with a little salt and peppercorns. Cover with water. Simmer until meat is just tender. Remove meat from pot. Cool. Wrap in foil. Chill overnight. Early the next day, cut meat and green pepper into julienne strips about 1 inch long. Combine with remaining ingredients. Toss lightly. Chill well before serving. Makes 6 servings.

SAUCE VINAIGRETTE

1 tbs. wine vinegar
3 tbs. olive oil
1/4 tsp. salt
few grains pepper
1/8 tsp. dry mustard
1/4 tsp. water
1-1/2 tsp. parsley
1/2 tsp. each dried chervil, chives, basil and marjoram

Combine in blender container. Cover. Blend on low speed 5 seconds only. Pour over salad ingredients. Toss lightly.

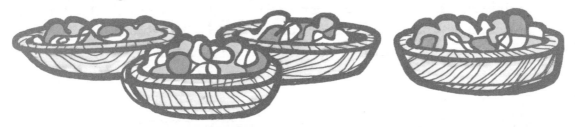

CHICKEN SALAD

6 tbs. butter	6 hard cooked eggs	3 tbs. tarragon vinegar
6 chicken breast halves	1/2 cup celery	salt, pepper, paprika
2 cups milk	6 tbs. olive oil	Sauce Mayonnaise, page 173

Stuff 1 tablespoon butter under the skin of each breast. Lay breasts skin side up in a roasting pan. Add milk. Bake in 375°F oven 30 minutes or until skin puffs and turns crispy brown. Baste frequently with milk. Remove breasts from pan. Chill. When breasts are chilled, remove skin. Cut meat into medium sized chunks. Slice eggs. Chop celery as fine as you possibly can. Carefully mix chicken, egg slices and celery together in large bowl. Combine olive oil, vinegar, salt, pepper and paprika in blender container. Cover. Blend on high speed until well mixed. Pour over chicken mixture. Allow to marinate several hours or overnight if possible. Make Sauce Mayonnaise as directed. Add enough to chicken to bind. Chill the salad thoroughly. Turn out on a bed of lettuce. Frost with a thin layer of Sauce Mayonnaise. Garnish with more sliced eggs and capers, if desired. Makes 6 servings.

134

TOMATO-AVOCADO-EGG-RED ONION SALAD

Another Paul Mayer original.

3 small tomatoes
3 hard cooked eggs
1 avocado, sliced
3 small red onions, thinly sliced
1-1/2 cups olive oil

1/2 cup tarragon vinegar
salt, black pepper
pinch dry mustard, paprika
1/4 tsp. marjoram
3 heads butter lettuce

Peel tomatoes and eggs. Cut each into eighths. Place in large mixing bowl with avocado and onion slices. Combine oil, vinegar, salt, pepper, mustard, paprika and marjoram in blender container. Cover. Blend on low speed 5 seconds. Pour over ingredients in bowl. Allow to marinate as long as possible. Wash and dry lettuce leaves well. Tear large ones if necessary. Arrange in salad bowl. Add marinated ingredients and dressing. Toss lightly until each leaf is coated with dressing. Serve. Makes 6 to 8 servings.

TOMATO AND HEARTS OF PALM SALAD

1 can hearts of palm
6 small tomatoes
1 pkg. (8 oz.) cream cheese
1 tbs. Kikkoman soy sauce
1 tbs. sherry
1/2 cup whipping cream
1/2 cup half & half
1 tbs. horseradish
1/2 tsp. each fenugreek, turmeric, cumin and ginger
salt, pepper, Tabasco, to taste

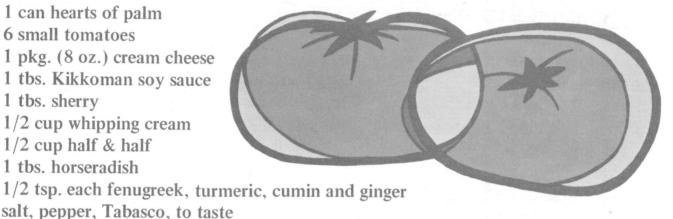

Drain hearts of palm. Cut each into 4 strips. Peel tomatoes. Cut into eighths. Chill thoroughly. Combine remaining ingredients in blender container. Cover. Blend on high speed until mixed. Chill. To serve arrange hearts of palm strips and tomato wedges alternately on salad plates. Spoon dressing over salad. Garnish with paprika. Makes 6 servings.

136

SALAD DE POMMES DE TERRE

2 lbs. tiny new red potatoes
salt, pepper
1/3 cup hot bouillon
1 tiny onion
1 tbs. white wine vinegar
3 tbs. olive oil

1/8 tsp. dry mustard
1/4 tsp. water
1-1/2 tbs. chopped parsley
1/2 tsp. each dried chervil,
   basil, tarragon

Peel and slice potatoes 1/2 inch thick. Cook in boiling salted water just until tender, 5 to 10 minutes. Do not overcook. Drain thoroughly. Place hot slices in mixing bowl. Season with salt and pepper. Add hot bouillon. Toss carefully until all liquid is absorbed. Place remaining ingredients in blender container. Cover. Blend on low speed 5 seconds. Pour over potato slices. Toss carefully. Serve at room temperature. Makes 4 to 6 servings.

SALADE DE HARICOTS VERTS DE TOMATES

6 tbs. olive oil
2 tbs. tarragon vinegar
salt, pepper, paprika
2 to 3 tbs. each chives, capers
2 to 3 tbs. seeded Kosher-style dill pickle
6 to 8 tomatoes
1 lb. French-cut green beans

Place oil, vinegar, salt, pepper, paprika, chives, capers and pickle in blender container. Cover. Blend on low speed 5 to 10 seconds, or until vegetables are chopped. Dip tomatoes in boiling water 15 seconds. Plunge into cold water immediately. Peel and hollow them out. Salt and invert to drain. Cook beans using the Paul Mayer Method, page 108. Drain and cool quickly in cold water. Drain thoroughly. Mix with dressing. Marinate as long as possible. Fill tomatoes with beans. Garnish with sprigs of parsley. Serve on bed of lettuce. Makes 6 to 8 servings.

MOLDED BEET RING

12 large beets
2 cups (1 pt.) sour cream
3 tbs. butter
2 tbs. horseradish
salt, black pepper

dash Tabasco
2 envelopes unflavored gelatine
1/2 cup cold water
sour cream, chives

Wash beets. Leave roots and about an inch of stem. Boil in salted water until tender. Skin. Cut beets into chunks. Place in blender container. Add sour cream, horseradish, salt, pepper and Tabasco. Cover. Blend on highest speed about 30 seconds or until well pureed. Sprinkle gelatine over water in small saucepan. Melt over low heat. Add to beet mixture. Cover. Blend 5 seconds on low speed. Spray a 5 cup ring mold with Pam. Pour in mixture. Chill. Unmold. Fill center with the salad of your choice. Pass a bowl of seasoned sour cream and chives. Makes 6 to 8 servings.

MOLDED CRAB SALAD

1 can (4 oz.) pimiento
1 egg
3/4 tsp. salt
1/2 tsp. dry mustard
1/4 tsp. paprika
1 tbs. white vinegar
1 cup salad oil

2 envelopes unflavored gelatine
1/2 cup cold water
1 small onion
2 stalks celery
1 lb. crab meat
onion salt, pepper, Tabasco, dill weed

Drain liquid from pimientos into blender container. Add egg, salt, mustard, paprika, vinegar and 1/4 cup of oil. Cover. Blend on highest speed. Remove cap from lid. Pour in 3/4 cup oil in a slow but steady stream. Beat only until mayonnaise is thick. Put mayonnaise in large bowl. Soften gelatin in water. Melt over hot water. Finely chop pimiento, onion and celery. Add chopped vegetables, crab meat and melted gelatine to mayonnaise. Season. Spray mold with Pam. Put mixture in mold. Chill. When firm, unmold and garnish. Makes 6 servings.

INSALATA DI MOZZARELLA

A restaurant in Milan served this one to me as a first course.

2 balls (1/2 lb. each) Mozzarella cheese
3 to 4 ripe unpeeled tomatoes
6 tbs. olive oil
2 tbs. red wine vinegar
salt, pepper
4 anchovy filets
1 tbs. basil

Cut cheese in 1/2 inch chunks. Remove entire center section of tomatoes. Cut remaining solid section into chunks the same size as the cheese. Place remaining ingredients in blender container. Cover. Blend on low speed 5 seconds or until anchovies have been chopped. Pour dressing over tomato-cheese mixture. Mix until thoroughly coated. Serve cool, but not chilled, either as is or on a bed of lettuce. Makes 6 to 8 servings.

Desserts

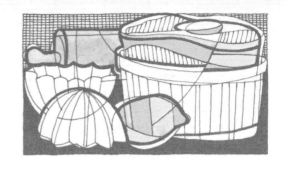

Although the following dessert recipes are all made easier through the use of the blender, they are as varied as one could imagine. There are light, elegant ones, old-fashioned steamed puddings and some unusual ones. All of them are delicious.

I have devoted an unusually large amount of space to the crepe—that universally enjoyed queen of the pancake dishes. A blender is its perfect companion, and its ability to be at home in almost any part of a meal makes it deserving of the space allotted. I have collected recipes for crepes from many restaurants throughout Europe. The outstanding dessert ones are included here.

All of the desserts are delightful treats which will add the proper finishing touch to your dinner menus. Most are served in small portions to accompany a demitasse of your favorite coffee.

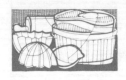

CHARLOTTE RUSSE

lady fingers
1 envelope unflavored gelatine
2 tbs. cold water
8 egg yolks

1 cup sugar
2 cups hot milk
2-inch piece vanilla bean, scraped
2 cups (1 pt.) whipping cream

Butter a Charlotte mold. Cover the bottom of mold completely with a design of triangular pieces of lady fingers. Line the side with upright lady fingers as close together as possible. Chill mold. Soak gelatine in water. Place egg yolks, sugar, milk and scrapings of vanilla bean in blender container. Cover. Blend on high speed 15 to 30 seconds. Pour into top of double boiler. Stir over simmering water until mixture coats the back of a spoon. Remove from hot water immediately. Stir in gelatine until completely dissolved. Transfer to a large metal bowl. Set in pan of ice water. Stir until cooled and beginning to set. Whip cream until stiff. Fold into cold custard. Pour mixture into chilled mold. Chill several hours or over night. To serve, unmold and decorate with whipped cream and maraschino cherries. Makes 10 to 12 servings.

LIQUEUR SOUFFLE

8 cup, well-buttered souffle dish	3/4 cup milk	6 tbs. liqueur*
3 tbs. butter	5 egg yolks	7 egg whites
3 tbs. flour	2 tbs. plus 2 tsp. sugar	

Preheat oven to 375°F. Sprinkle dish with a little sugar. Tie a collar of buttered waxed paper around rim of dish. Place butter, flour and milk in blender container. Cover. Blend on high speed 15 to 30 seconds. Pour into small saucepan. Stir over moderate heat until mixture thickens and boils. Remove from heat. Combine egg yolks with 2 tablespoons sugar. Rapidly beat into sauce. Add liqueur. Transfer to a large bowl. Beat egg whites until stiff but not dry. Add 2 teaspoons sugar. Beat 30 seconds. Fold into liqueur base. Pour into prepared dish. Bake in preheated oven 20 to 22 minutes.

*Use any liqueur or combination of liqueurs you wish. Some good combinations are creme de banan and white creme de menthe; apricot and raspberry; white creme de cacao and Cherry Heering; white creme de cacao and Grand Marnier.

145

CHOCOLATE SOUFFLE

Chocolate souffles do not, as a rule, rise quite as high as other kinds. One-third the depth out of the dish is considered a success.

6 cup, well-buttered souffle dish	3 tbs. flour
2 oz. bitter chocolate	1/2 cup sugar
3/4 cup milk	5 egg yolks
3 tbs. butter	7 egg whites

Preheat oven to 375°F. Sprinkle buttered dish with a little sugar. Melt chocolate in milk over low heat. Pour into blender container. Add butter, flour and 6 tablespoons sugar. Blend on high speed until everything is well blended. Pour into saucepan. Stir over moderate heat until sauce just begins to thicken. Remove from heat. Rapidly beat in egg yolks all at once. Transfer mixture to large bowl. Beat egg whites until stiff. Add remaining sugar. Continue beating 30 seconds. Fold into base. Pour into prepared dish. Bake in preheated oven 18 minutes. Serve at once.

BLANCMANGE

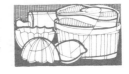

1 cup blanched almonds
2 to 3 drops almond extract
1-1/2 envelopes unflavored gelatine

1 cup (1/2 pt.) whipping cream
1/2 cup sugar
2 tbs. Kirsch or rum

Place almonds, extract and 2 tablespoons water in blender container. Cover. Blend on moderate speed until almonds are pulverized. Remove cap from lid. Gradually add 2 cups water with blender running. Line a sieve with a clean kitchen towel. Set sieve in bowl. Pour mixture into sieve. Gather up folds of towel. Squeeze until all almond water has been forced through. Set water aside until needed. Soften gelatine in 1/4 cup cold water. Dissolve over low heat. Combine almond water, whipping cream and sugar. Add to gelatine. Continue heating mixture until hot enough to dissolve sugar. Do not boil. Remove from heat. Set in pan of ice water until it is cool to the touch. Add Kirsch or rum. Pour into oiled ring mold. Refrigerate overnight. To serve, unmold onto large serving dish. Fill center with whole strawberries which have been marinated in Kirsch, rum or brandy. Makes 6 servings.

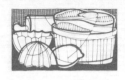

STEAMED CHOCOLATE PUDDING

2 oz. bitter chocolate	1 cup flour
1 egg	1 tsp. baking powder
1/2 cup sugar	1/8 tsp. salt
1 tbs. butter	1/2 cup milk
1 tbs. red current jelly	Vanilla Rum Sauce, page 149

Melt chocolate over lowest heat or hot, not boiling, water. Pour into blender with remaining ingredients. Cover. Blend on low speed 30 seconds to one minute or until ingredients are well mixed. Pour batter into well-greased pudding mold. (I like Crisco for greasing). If you are an optimist, grease the inside of the lid as well. Seal the mold tightly. Stand on a rack in a large kettle. Add as much boiling water as possible without having mold float. Steam for one hour. Add boiling water as necessary to keep level of water up. Unmold on a platter. Serve with Vanilla Rum Sauce.

VANILLA RUM SAUCE

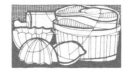

6 egg yolks
1 cup half and half
1 cup whipping cream
1 teaspoon vanilla
1/4 cup rum
1/2 cup sugar

Measure all ingredients into blender container. Cover. Blend on high speed 10 to 15 seconds or until well mixed. Pour into top of double boiler. Cook over, but not touching, boiling water. Stir constantly until mixture thickens. Remove from hot water. Set pan in ice water until warm. Keep warm for serving.

STEAMED SUET PUDDING

6 slices white bread
2 eggs
1 cup milk
1 cup firmly packed dark brown sugar
1/4 cup Sherry
2 tsp. vanilla
kidney suet
1 cup flour

1 tsp. baking soda
1 tsp. salt
1-1/2 tsp. cinnamon
1 tsp. each cloves and nutmeg
1/2 tsp. ginger
1 pkg. (15 oz.) light raisins
1/2 cup finely chopped candied fruit
1/2 cup chopped pecans

Break slices of bread into small pieces. Put into blender container. Add eggs, milk, brown sugar, sherry and vanilla. Cover. Blend on low speed 10 to 15 seconds. Trim skin and membrane from enough kidney suet to yield 2 firmly packed cupfuls. Add to blender. Cover. Blend on high speed until suet is well broken up. Help suet into blades with rubber scraper, so it breaks up evenly. Sift dry ingredients together. Add raisins, candied fruit and pecans. Toss to coat with flour. Add blender ingredients. Stir only until mixed. Turn into well greased 8 to

10 cup ring mold. Cover tightly. Place on rack in large kettle. Add boiling water and steam as described in the previous recipe. Steam 3-1/2 hours. Add boiling water as needed. Lift pudding from water. Remove lid. Allow to stand 10 minutes before turning out. To serve, blaze with brandy. Serve with pure, sweet cream.

Note: For a smaller pudding cut ingredients in half. Steam in a 1 quart mold, 1 hour and 15 minutes. Allow to stand, as described, before turning out.

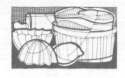

GINGER ROLL

1 jellyroll pan	1/2 cup hot water
1/3 cup melted butter	1 cup flour
1/3 cup light corn syrup	1 tsp. each ginger, cinnamon, nutmeg, allspice
1/3 cup dark molasses	1 tsp. baking soda
1 whole egg	

Grease the 11 x 15 inch pan with Crisco. Line with waxed paper. Grease paper. Measure ingredients into blender container in order listed. Cover. Blend on low speed 15 to 25 seconds or until thoroughly blended and smooth. Do not over blend. Pour into prepared pan. Bake in 350°F oven 15 minutes, or until cake is just set and pulls slightly away from the edges of the pan. Take care not to overbake or it will crack when rolled. Remove from oven. Cover surface closely with a damp towel. Place in refrigerator immediately to cool. When the bottom of pan feels cool, sprinkle top of cake with confectioners' sugar. Carefully turn it out onto overlapping sheets of waxed paper. Spread with stiffly whipped cream which has been sweetened and flavored. Roll up lengthwise and dust with more sugar.

CREPES

Probably one of the most universal of dishes, and also one of the most universally enjoyed, is the pancake. Griddlecakes, flapjacks, buckwheats, blintzes, blinis, you name it, all are made from batter baked on a flat open pan as a prelude to being filled with cheese, creamed seafood or poultry, applesauce, sour cream, vegetables, once again you name it. They are eaten with butter, maple syrup, bacon, ham, and so many other accompaniments that it's only, really, a question of just how imaginative one is that determines the mode of serving. Of them all, undeniably the queen of the frying pan cake is the crepe.

Almost every recipe for crepes which I have seen has stipulated that the batter must rest at least 30 minutes before beginning to make the pancakes. Not so when made with a blender, I have discovered! The pancakes produced in the following fashion come out light, well-textured, and tender. They may be made well in advance of the time at which they are to be finished, and stored one on top of the other, with nothing in between them. The best way is on a wooden board with a large bowl inverted over them. Similarly stacked they may be wrapped in aluminum foil, and frozen. The only word of caution here is to be sure that you

154

allow them to thaw completely before trying to separate them.

Now! Just a word or two about making the crepes! How easy that sounds! And easy it really is, if you observe one or two rules. First and foremost! Reserve a pan exclusively for making them! DO NOT WASH IT EVER! A teflon pan will do admirably, but it, too, should never be washed, merely wiped clean with paper toweling after each use. If you are using a metal pan, one made of cast iron or cast aluminum is best, and it should be treated before its first use in the following manner: Spread the surface of the pan with vegetable oil, and allow the pan to rest in this fashion for 24 hours. Then, with the oil still in the pan, heat it until it smokes. Turn off the heat and with the oil remaining in the pan allow the pan to cool until it is completely cold. Then, pour off the oil, and wipe the pan dry with paper toweling. Your pan should then be ready for the first crepe. If it should stick at this point, retreat it as above, try again until you make a crepe that will not stick. After that, provided some well-meaning soul doesn't do you a favor and wash your pan, you should have no further troubles. Just follow the basic recipe and directions on page 156.

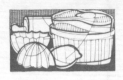

BLENDER CREPES

When making dessert crepes, increase sugar to 3 tablespoons.

1-1/2 cups milk
3 eggs
grated rind of 1/2 lemon
1 tsp. sugar
3 tbs. butter, cooled
3 tbs. brandy
7/8 cup flour*

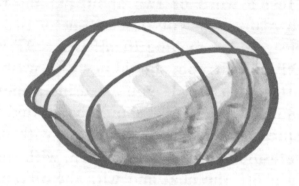

Measure ingredients into blender container in the order listed. Cover. Blend on medium speed only as long as necessary to mix everything well, about 15 to 30 seconds. Pour batter into bowl. Cook crepes in the following manner:

Butter a 5 or 6 inch skillet lightly, for the first crepe only. Tip pan and slowly pour in crepe batter, just coating bottom of pan, about 2 tablespoons. Tilt the pan immediately so that the batter will completely spread over the entire bottom

156

of the pan. Cook quickly on moderate heat until edges begin to brown. Loosen around edges with a thin spatula. Grasp crepe firmly with both hands and flip it over. Cook on reverse side 5 seconds only. Turn crepe out onto plate. Continue cooking crepes without adding butter to pan, until all batter is used. If you are especially adept it is possible to use two crepe pans at once, filling one and then the other, and finally turning them out in the same order, leaving you two empty crepe pans with which to begin again.

Using a small crepe pan and a minimum amount of batter for each crepe, the basic recipe should yield 18 to 24 crepes. Once you have mastered the process of making the little fellows, make them often. Serve with super fillings and sauce and delight your guests and family with crepes, crepes and more crepes. The crepes themselves freeze perfectly. Make them ahead and keep on hand at all times. Leftovers wrapped in a crepe and served with a delicious sauce, become a beautifully disguised entree.

*Measure 1 cup, remove 2 tablespoons.

CREPES ADVOCKAAT

Advockaat is an egg nog flavored cordial made in Holland.

Blender Crepes, page 156
3 oranges or
1 can (11 oz.) mandarin oranges
juice of 1/2 lemon

3 tbs. sugar
2 oz. raspberry liqueur
2 oz. Chartreuse
1/2 cup Advockaat

Prepare crepes as directed. Keep warm. Peel and section oranges or, drain and dry mandarin sections. Combine lemon juice and sugar in the blazing pan of a chafing dish or large skillet. When sugar is melted and begins to caramelize, add raspberry liqueur and Chartreuse. Heat and ignite. When flame dies, add oranges. Allow mixture to reduce until it becomes sticky. Add Advockaat. Re-ignite the mixture, if it will still flame. Allow to bubble and thicken slightly. Fold crepes into quarters. Place two or three on each dessert plate. Spoon on sauce. Serve immediately. Makes 6 to 8 servings.

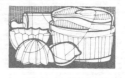

Gervais is a brand of French cream cheese readily available in most speciality cheese shops. Philadelphia Brand is an acceptable substitute.

Blender Crepes, page 156
1 pkg. (3 oz.) Gervais
Apricot liqueur
granulated sugar
2 to 3 tbs. Scotch whisky, warmed

Beat together Gervais (or other cream cheese) and enough apricot liqueur to make a thick but spreadable cream. The mixture should have enough liqueur in it to be smooth and shiny. Spread each crepe with some of the cream mixture. Roll up. Place the filled crepes tightly against one another in serving dish. Sprinkle with sugar. (At this point you may keep them warm in the oven for as long as you wish). Just before serving, sprinkle with warmed Scotch and ignite. Serve crepes while still ablaze. Makes 6 servings.

159

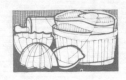

CREPES SOUFFLES

Whoever first got the idea of combining the two lightest desserts in the world must have been someone with a truly delicate sense of propriety, because there really is something ethereal about the blending of the souffle and the crepe.

Blender Crepes, page 156
Liqueur Souffle batter, page 145
confectioners sugar

Make crepes as directed. Allow 3 per serving. Prepare souffle batter. Preheat oven to 375°F. When ready to serve, lay crepes flat. Place a spoonful of souffle batter at the edge of each crepe. Fold in half once to cover batter. Fold again into quarters, in such a fashion that three of the quarters are beneath the souffle batter—only one is on top. Lift crepes onto lightly greased baking sheet. Bake in preheated oven 10 minutes or until souffle has risen and forced top layer of crepe open. Arrange on serving plate quickly. Sprinkle with confectioners sugar. Speed to the table. Makes 6 to 8 servings.

160

CREPES MEXICAINE

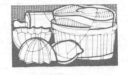

I was served this bit of ambrosia at the Hotel Prinses Juliana in Valeknburg, Netherlands. The weather was horrible but the food was out of this world!

Blender Crepes, page 156
2-1/2 tbs. fine sugar
1/2 cup strong, fresh coffee
1 tsp. instant coffee
3 to 4 drops lemon juice

2 oz. Kahlua
2 oz. Kirsch
coffee flavored ice cream
whipped cream
sliced toasted almonds

Make crepes as directed. Fold into quarters. Melt sugar in the blazing pan of a chafing dish. Add coffee slowly so it boils without stopping. Add instant coffee and lemon juice. Place folded crepes in blazing pan. Pour Kahlua over them. Ignite. When flame goes out add Kirsch. Ignite again. Remove crepes from pan. Open and fill each one with softened ice cream. Close again over ice cream. Place on dessert plates. Spoon sauce over each one. Garnish with whipped cream and almonds. Makes 6 to 8 servings.

CREPES SIR HOLDAN

I haven't the foggiest notion who Sir Holdan was!

Blender Crepes, page 156
1 cup (1/2 pt.) sour cream
2 tbs. white creme de cacao
vanilla ice cream
2 tbs. sweet butter

1/2 cup raspberries
juice 1/2 lemon
2 tbs. Kirsch
2 tbs. Cognac
toasted sliced almonds

Prepare crepes as directed. Combine sour cream and creme de cacao. Fill crepes with ice cream. Quickly melt butter in the blazing pan of a chafing dish, or in a large skillet. Add raspberries and lemon juice. Pour in Kirsch and ignite. When flame goes out, add Cognac and ignite. Stir until flame goes out and juice is cooked away from the berries. Place the crepes on dessert plates. Top with a spoonful of raspberry sauce, then a spoonful of sour cream. Top with almonds. Serve immediately. Makes 6 to 8 servings.

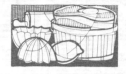

CREPES SUZETTE

Blender Crepes, page 156
12 lumps sugar
2 oranges
1/3 cup sweet butter
3 oz. Grand Marnier
4 oz. fine brandy

Prepare crepes according to directions. Rub sugar lumps over orange skins to absorb zest. Then squeeze juice from oranges. Melt butter in the blazing pan of a chafing dish. Add orange juice and sugar lumps. Heat until mixture is bubbling and sugar has dissolved. Add Grand Marnier. Ignite. Spoon the liquid up to aerate the liqueur. Continue until flame goes out. Bathe each crepe in sauce before folding into quarters. Pull crepes to one side of pan. Add brandy, and ignite. Baste crepes with flaming sauce and if possible serve while still blazing. Allow 3 crepes for each serving. Makes 6 servings.

Sauces

The blender is a great time saver in sauce making. Difficult to make egg-based sauces become easy and almost fool-proof. And, when making cream sauces, all ingredients are blended together a few seconds then poured into a saucepan and quickly cooked as directed. Because of the complete success of these methods, I probably use my blender more for saucemaking than for any other one purpose.

There are literally thousands of sauces, all of which stem from a basic few much in the manner of a family tree. The great French chefs would undoubtedly be horrified at the thought of taking shortcuts with their creations, yet this is precisely what we shall do with these blender sauce recipes which are true gourmet delights. I have gathered together my favorites and those which I think you will use most often. After you have tried them, I hope you will use the blender to make your own favorites this easy new way.

SAUCE BECHAMEL

2 tbs. butter
2 tbs. flour
2-1/2 cups milk
pinch powdered thyme
pinch nutmeg
salt, cayenne pepper
small bay leaf

Place butter, flour, milk, thyme, nutmeg, salt and cayenne in blender container. Cover. Blend on high speed 15 to 30 seconds. Pour into saucepan. Cook over moderate heat, stirring constantly, until mixture comes to a boil. Add bay leaf. Lower heat. Simmer 45 minutes or until sauce is thickened and reduced to 1 cup. Strain. Use as is or as directed in other recipes. Makes 1 cup.

This subtle delicate sauce is delicious over poached fish, eggs and salmon.

1 cup Sauce Bechamel, page 166
1/2 lb. medium sized shrimp
white wine
salt

1/2 cup (1/4 lb.) butter, melted
1/4 cup whipping cream
1 tbs. brandy
dash cayenne pepper

Reduce Sauce Bechamel over low heat until it measures 1/2 cup. Cover with plastic wrap pressed tightly against surface of the sauce. Set aside. Cook shrimp by first barely covering them with equal amounts of water and wine. Add a little salt. Bring to full boil. Remove shrimp from pan. Cool quickly under cold running water. Boil cooking liquid down to 2 tablespoons. Blend into the thickened Bechamel. Shell shrimp. Put shells into blender container with melted butter. Run on low speed 30 to 60 seconds, or until shells are pulverized. Strain through fine sieve or cheesecloth. Add 6 tablespoons of the shrimp butter, whipping cream, brandy and cayenne to sauce. Mix thoroughly.

SAUCE CHAUDFROID

Chaudfroid Sauce is used for coating anything cold, but mainly meats, poultry and fish. It is sometimes tinted with food coloring or saffron.

1/4 cup butter	2 cups chicken broth	2 envelopes unflavored gelatine
1/4 cup flour	salt, cayenne pepper	1/3 cup cold water
		1 cup (1/2 pt.) whipping cream

Measure butter, flour, broth, salt and cayenne into blender container. Cover. Blend on high speed 15 to 30 seconds. Pour into saucepan. Stir over moderate heat until mixture comes to a boil. Lower heat. Cook gently 30 minutes. Stir occasionally. Soften gelatine in cold water 5 to 10 minutes. Place over hot water until melted. When sauce has cooked 30 minutes, remove from heat. Strain. Add gelatine. Stir to thoroughly blend. Gradually add cream. Stir over ice water to cool. Use when just beginning to thicken. If sauce begins to set before it has all been used, melt again by placing bowl in hot water for a minute. Makes about 2 cups.

SAUCE SUPREME GOURMET

1/3 cup butter
1/3 cup flour
3 cups chicken stock
1/2 tsp. salt
cayenne pepper
4 egg yolks

2/3 cup hot cream
6 tbs. sherry
1-1/2 tbs. finely chopped truffles
1/2 tsp. paprika
2 tsp. lemon juice

Measure butter, flour, stock, salt, and cayenne into blender container. Cover. Blend 15 to 30 seconds. Pour into saucepan. Stir over moderate heat until mixture boils. Lower heat. Continue cooking until sauce reduces to about 2 cups and is thick and creamy. Stir only occassionally to prevent scorching. Return to blender. Add eggs and cream. Cover. Blend on low speed 15 to 20 seconds. Add sherry. If sauce is too thin at this point, return to saucepan. Heat carefully, without boiling, until thickened. Stir constantly. Adjust seasonings. Stir in truffles, paprika and lemon juice. (Lemon juice may be increased to as much as 4 tablespoons. Use your own preference as a guide.) Makes 4 to 6 servings.

SAUCE MORNAY

A bed of cooked spinach, poached eggs and golden Sauce Mornay, run under the broiler to glaze and brown the sauce, and you have Poached Eggs Florentine. The star of the production is this really grand and rich sauce.

2 tbs. butter

2 tbs. flour

1 cup cream

salt, cayenne pepper

1/2 cup Gruyere cheese

2 tbs. Parmesan cheese

dry mustard

2 egg yolks

Measure butter, flour, cream, salt and cayenne into blender container. Cover. Blend on high speed for 15 to 30 seconds. Add Gruyere and Parmesan. Blend 15 seconds. Pour into saucepan. Cook, stirring, until mixture comes to boil. Add a pinch of dry mustard. (Do not worry if sauce separates at this point.) Return to blender container. Add egg yolks. Cover. Blend on high speed until smooth and shiny. Keep warm over hot, but not boiling, water. Press plastic wrap down against surface to exclude all air and prevent top from drying. Makes about 1-1/2 cups.

SAUCE HOLLANDAISE

2 egg yolks

salt, cayenne pepper, to taste

1 to 2 tbs. lemon juice

1/2 cup (1/4 lb.) butter, melted

Place egg yolks, lemon juice, salt and cayenne in blender. Cover. Blend on low speed 5 seconds. Remove cap. Pour in butter, in a slow steady stream. Continue blending only until sauce has thickened. (Should it curdle, add 2 additional egg yolks. Blend at high speed while adding whipping cream 1 tablespoon at a time until sauce reconstitutes.) Makes about 1 cup.

SAUCE CHANTILLY

A lighter, ethereal version of Sauce Hollandaise.

1/2 cup whipping cream

1 cup Sauce Hollandaise

Whip cream until stiff. Gently fold into Hollandaise.

171

SAUCE BEARNAISE

For grilled meats, serve Hollandaise's first cousin.

4 shallots
1/2 cup tarragon vinegar
2 egg yolks
salt

cayenne pepper
1 tsp. each parsley, chives, tarragon
1/2 cup (1/4 lb.) melted butter, cooled

Place shallots and vinegar in blender container. Cover. Run blender on low speed 10 to 15 seconds or until shallots are chopped. Pour mixture into small saucepan. Reduce until it measures 2 tablespoons. Strain out shallots. Pour strained vinegar back into blender container. Add egg yolks, salt, cayenne, parsley, chives and tarragon. Cover. Blend on lowest speed. Remove cap, not cover. Gradually pour in cooled butter. As soon as sauce thickens, stop blending. Makes about 3/4 cup.

SAUCE MAYONNAISE

3 whole eggs
2-1/4 tsp. salt
1-1/2 tsp. dry mustard
pinch paprika

6 tbs. white vinegar <u>or</u>
6 tbs. lemon juice <u>or</u>
3 tbs. of each
3-1/2 cups oil

Place eggs, salt, mustard, paprika, vinegar (or lemon juice) and 3/4 cup oil in blender container. Cover. Blend on highest speed 5 seconds or until mixed. Remove cap from cover. Start adding oil in a slow but steady stream. Pour directly into the center of the whirlpool formed by the swirling mixture. Pour steadily until the whirlpool disappears completely. This should use 1-1/2 to 2 cups of the oil. Continue adding oil, a little at a time. The mayonnaise will become thicker and thicker. Add the oil in this manner until it is all gone. Never add more oil until each addition is completely worked in. Keep blender on highest speed all the time. Makes 1 quart.

SAUCE MAYONNAISE RAVIGOTE

For a change try this one with beautifully crisp fried fish instead of tartar sauce—you'll never go back.

2 tbs. each capers, chervil, parsley, shallots and onion
1/4 cup dry white wine
1 tbs. strained lemon juice
1/2 tsp. anchovy paste
1 hard-cooked egg white, finely chopped
1 cup Sauce Mayonnaise

Measure capers, chervil, parsley, shallots, onion, wine and lemon juice into blender container. Blend on low speed about 10 seconds. Pour mixture into sauce pan. Cook very gently 15 minutes. Pour into a large bowl. Cool. Add anchovy paste and egg white. Beat in mayonnaise. Chill thoroughly before serving. Makes about 1-1/2 cups.

SAUCE MAYONNAISE CHAUDFROID

Mayonnaise can also be used chaudfroid for coating hard boiled eggs, fish, and most of the things you would coat with regular Sauce Chaudfroid. Chicken salad takes on a glistening, professional appearance when coated with Mayonnaise Chaudfroid and garnished with capers and hard cooked egg slices.

2 envelopes unflavored gelatine   2 cups Sauce Mayonnaise, page 173
1/2 cup cold water

Sprinkle gelatine over cold water in small saucepan. Place over lowest possible heat. Heat, stirring, until it is fluid and completely melted. Measure mayonnaise into bowl. Quickly stir in melted gelatine, using wire whip to blend thoroughly. Use the chaudfroid at once or it will set. Should it do so, place the bowl briefly in warm water. Stir until sauce becomes spreadable once again. Place coated item in the refrigerator to set. Once it has set, it will stay firm without being kept on ice. However, avoid placing to close to candles or in direct sunlight. Makes about 2-1/2 cups.

TOMATO SAUCE

3 tbs. butter
3 tbs. flour
1 can (16 oz.) stewed tomatoes
1 can (6 oz.) tomato paste
1 clove garlic
sugar
salt, pepper to taste
1/2 cup whipping cream

Put butter, flour, tomatoes, tomato paste, garlic, pinch of sugar, salt and pepper in blender container. Cover. Blend on high speed until smooth. Pour into saucepan. Stir over moderate heat until mixture comes to a boil. Remove from heat. Stir in whipping cream and another pinch of sugar. Reheat, but do not boil. Serve immediately. Makes about 2-1/4 cups.

SAUCE JOINVILLE

Whenever wine, water and seasonings are used to poach fish, drain and use the poaching liquid to make this delicious sauce.

2 tbs. butter
1 tbs. flour
1-1/2 cups poaching liquid

1/2 cup cream
2 egg yolks
6 tbs. Shrimp-Lobster Butter, page 179

Measure butter, flour and poaching liquid into blender container. Cover. Run on high speed 15 to 30 seconds. Pour into saucepan. Stir over medium heat until mixture boils. Lower heat. Allow sauce to reduce 20 to 25 minutes or until nicely thickened. Return to blender container. Add cream and egg yolks. Cover. Blend on low speed 10 seconds or until egg yolks are well mixed and sauce thickens still further. Reduce remaining poaching liquid to 1 teaspoon. Combine reduced liquid, Shrimp-Lobster Butter and sauce. Serve with poached fish. Makes 4 to 6 servings.

shells from 1/2 lb. cooked shrimp
shells from 2 small cooked lobster tails
1/4 cup melted butter

Put shells into blender container with butter. Cover. Blend on high speed 10 to 15 seconds or until shells are pulverized and blended with butter. Strain through cheesecloth or fine sieve. Use as directed.

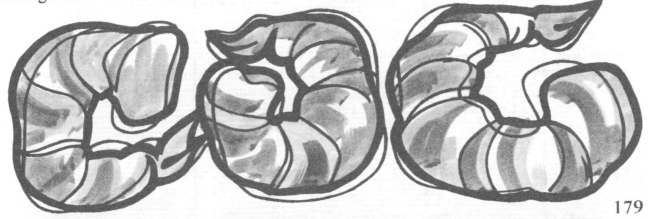

Index